Celebration
COCKTAILS

Quarto.com

© 2025 Quarto Publishing Group USA Inc.
Text © 2025 Rhiannon Lee
Photography © 2025 Georgie Glass

First Published in 2025 by The Harvard Common Press, an imprint of The Quarto Group,
100 Cummings Center, Suite 265-D, Beverly, MA 01915, USA.
T (978) 282-9590 F (978) 283-2742

The Harvard Common Press titles are also available at discount for retail, wholesale,
promotional, and bulk purchase. For details, contact the Special Sales Manager by email
at specialsales@quarto.com or by mail at The Quarto Group, Attn: Special Sales Manager,
100 Cummings Center, Suite 265-D, Beverly, MA 01915, USA.

29 28 27 26 25   1 2 3 4 5

ISBN: 978-0-7603-9948-4

Digital edition published in 2025   ˙
eISBN: 978-0-7603-9949-1

Library of Congress Cataloging-in-Publication Data is available.

Cover Images: bottom left, Georgie Glass, all others: Shutterstock
Photography: Georgie Glass
Drink Stylist: Sarah Hancox, Grace Hatley (page 133)

Printed in China

Celebration COCKTAILS

Outstanding Batch Cocktails and Individual
Drinks for Holidays, Parties, Birthdays,
Weddings, and Other Festive Occasions

RHIANNON LEE

HARVARD
COMMON
PRESS

This book is dedicated to all
my friends and family who
have celebrated the good
times and great memories
throughout the years.
Cheers to your love and
support, and may we all
have many more reasons to
celebrate in the future.

Contents

CHAPTER 1

Winter Cheers & Cozy Celebrations 45

CHAPTER 2

Spring Sips & Garden Gatherings 71

CHAPTER 3

Summer Breezes & Sunset Parties 87

CHAPTER 4

Autumn Alchemy & Harvest Festivities 109

CHAPTER 5

Anytime Occasions: Milestones & Merriment 127

Special Occasions Call for Special Drinks

LIFE IS FULL OF MOMENTS that deserve to be celebrated—whether it's a significant achievement, a meaningful milestone, or simply a cherished holiday with family and friends. These magical moments not only bring joy and laughter, but they also create lasting memories and stories that stay with us for a lifetime. Perhaps it's the memory of a great aunt having one too many sherries at Christmas and attempting to get on a pogo stick, or the unforgettable scene of a college roommate's twenty-first birthday, when their first taste of tequila sparked some "creative" dance moves. It's these moments (and the drinks that help fuel them) that we cherish and recount year after year.

To help create even more of these unforgettable moments, this book is your ultimate guide to pairing every special occasion, whether it's a big blowout or an intimate anniversary with a signature cocktail that is festive, delicious, and perfectly suited to the event.

Get ready to become the host with the most, because your gatherings are about to reach a whole new level. A well-crafted cocktail has the power to transform an ordinary event into something extraordinary. Each drink in this book is not only visually stunning and Instagram-worthy but also a great way to spark conversation, get people mixing, and set the stage for unforgettable moments of merriment.

This book is divided by seasons, taking you through the year and beyond, offering cocktails that capture the spirit of each season's most memorable occasions. Start with the cozy warmth of winter—sip a Gingerbread Martini (see page 48) while unwrapping Christmas gifts by the tree, or enjoy a romantic Vodka-Soaked Valentine's (see page 58), a sophisticated pink drink that's perfect for a February 14 date night.

With the arrival of spring, new opportunities to celebrate fresh beginnings are plentiful. Picture yourself savoring a Blossom Breeze (see page 74) to mark the first cherry blossoms, or indulging in an Easter Eggstravaganza (see page 77)—a decadent Irish cream liqueur-infused cocktail served inside a hollow chocolate egg, perfect for indulging during the holiday.

As summer arrives, so does a wealth of reasons to raise a glass. From lively Pride events to picnics, BBQs, and garden parties, the occasions to celebrate are endless. Toast your summer vacation with a Tropical Getaway (see page 92), bursting with exotic fruit flavors, or raise a glass to the longest day of the year with a refreshing Sunshine Sangria (see page 91), perfect for serving at sun-drenched alfresco dinner parties with friends.

When fall rolls in, embrace the season with cozy, spiced cocktails that warm you from the inside out, or get into the spirit of the season with some playful, spooky concoctions. Whether it's a Witches' Brew (see page 121) or Zombie-Brain Shots (see page 118), these fun and eerie libations will be the ultimate treat—no trick—at any Halloween celebration.

The final chapter celebrates life's most significant milestones—engagement parties, housewarmings, birthdays, and more. No matter the occasion, there's always a perfect drink to raise a glass to love, success, and new beginnings.

Whether you're a novice or a seasoned mixologist, *Celebration Cocktails* makes crafting exceptional drinks easy and approachable. With a guide to essential techniques, an overview of glassware, and a glossary of key mixology terms, you'll quickly gain the confidence to create cocktails that wow.

Perfect for party hosts and cocktail enthusiasts alike, this book will become your go-to companion for raising spirits and making every occasion unforgettable. Stock your bar cart, grab your shaker, and get ready to toast life's most remarkable moments. With *Celebration Cocktails*, there's a signature drink for every season and every reason to celebrate.

Mixology Measurements

When crafting cocktails, precision in measurement is essential, but it can also be a bit confusing, especially with all the different terms used. Whether you're following a classic recipe or creating your own concoction, it's important to understand what each term means in terms of volume. Here's a quick guide to common cocktail measurement terms, both in Imperial and metric equivalents.

Term	U.S. Imperial Measurement	Metric Equivalent
1 part	Varies (relative measure)	Varies (relative measure)
Dash	⅛ teaspoon	0.6 milliliters
Teaspoon	⅕ ounce	5 milliliters
Tablespoon	½ ounce	15 milliliters
Shot	1 ounce	30 milliliters
Snit	3 ounces	90 milliliters
Split	6 ounces	175 milliliters
Cup	8 ounces	235 milliliters
Pint	16 ounces	475 milliliters

Cocktail Equipment

To ensure cocktails are always a hit, it's essential to master the basics of cocktail equipment. With the right tools and techniques, anyone can create delightful drinks that taste great and impress guests. Fortunately, high-end equipment isn't necessary; just following these tips and tricks can lead to cocktail perfection. Here are the essential tools that will help mix, shake, and stir the way to memorable celebrations.

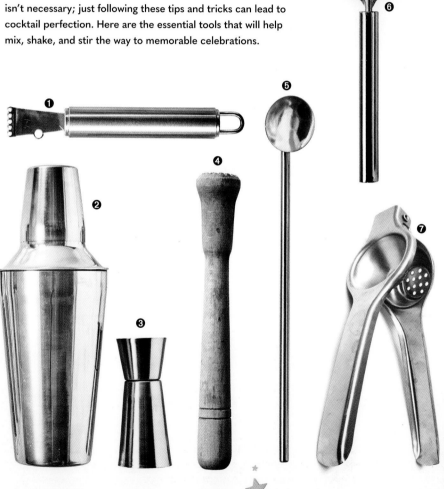

1. Peeler and Zester

While a knife can be used, a peeler is more efficient for creating uniform citrus garnishes with minimal pith. Both peel and zest are common components in many cocktails, making these tools quite handy.

BARTENDER TIP: Lightly squeeze a citrus peel over a flame to release more oils, then pass it over the drink.

2. Cocktail Shaker

Coming in all different shapes and sizes, the standard shaker is stainless steel with three parts: a base known as a "can," a built-in strainer, and a cap (which can be used as a jigger). It's brilliantly straightforward and easy to keep clean. If you can't get hold of a cocktail shaker, consider using a large glass jar with a lid and a waterproof seal.

3. Jigger/Shot Glass

Something to measure your proportions with is a toolbox essential for any avid cocktail maker. The jigger is the standard measure for spirits and liqueurs. If you don't have a jigger, a single shot glass or even an eggcup can be a stand-in. In this book, one shot is measured as 1 ounce (30 ml). (See page 15 for unit conversions).

4. Muddler

To extract maximum flavor from certain fresh garnishes, such as mint or fruit, a muddler is used to crush the ingredients. If a muddler is not available, a fork can be used—with gentle pressure—as a substitute.

5. Bar Spoon

The classic bar spoon features a long, twisted handle, a flat end, and a teardrop-shaped spoon, ideal for measuring and stirring spirits

6. Strainer

Most cocktail shakers are sold with a built-in strainer. However, if yours doesn't have one, then a flour sieve works just as well.

BARTENDER TIP: When a cocktail calls for straining, ensure you've used full ice cubes, as crushed ice tends to clog the strainer in standard shakers.

7. Citrus Squeezer

A citrus squeezer is an essential tool for efficiently extracting juice from fresh citrus fruits. If you don't have one, you can use your hands along with a fork to extract every last drop of juice.

BARTENDER TIP: To get the most juice, roll the fruit in the palm of your hands then slice

it in half and microwave for 5 seconds. Then simply use a fork to press and twist for maximum yield.

8. Blender

An electric blender is necessary for recipes that involve blending fruit and ice cubes. It does not need to be a high-end model; a basic blender capable of crushing ice will suffice.

❽

Techniques

From mastering the art of twisting citrus garnishes to delicately layering ingredients for that Instagram-worthy gradient effect, here is a guide to the techniques needed to shake, layer, and stir your way to cocktail perfection.

Shake

When a cocktail includes eggs, fruit juice, or cream, it's essential to shake all the ingredients. This process not only mixes them thoroughly but also aerates and chills the drink. While there's no consensus on the exact shaking time, a good rule of thumb is to shake vigorously until the shaker feels cool to the touch.

Layer

Also known as building, this technique involves carefully pouring ingredients over the back of a spoon to create distinct layers. It's often used for visually striking cocktails like the B-52.

BARTENDER TIP: Always start with the heaviest liquid (with the most sugar content).

Stir

Used for spirit-forward cocktails like the martini or Manhattan, stirring gently combines ingredients without diluting them too much. It maintains the clarity and smooth texture of the drink.

BARTENDER TIP: Stir your drink with a bar spoon until condensation forms on the outside of the glass—this indicates it's perfectly chilled and ready to serve.

Rim

To add an elegant touch to your cocktail, you can decorate the rim of the glass with various ingredients like salt, sugar, cinnamon, and edible glitter. To achieve this, spread a few tablespoons of the desired ingredient onto a small plate. Moisten the outer rim of the glass with a citrus wedge, water, or a syrup, then roll the outer rim of the glass on the plate until lightly coated. Hold the glass upside down and tap to release any excess.

Twist

Some cocktails call for a citrus twist to garnish a cocktail. This is a simple way to make a cocktail look elegant, but it also adds citrus notes to the aroma of the drink. Use a sharp paring knife to cut a thin, oval disk of the peel, avoiding the pith (the white spongy part). Gently grasp the outer edges skin-side down between the thumb and two fingers, then pinch the twist over the drink. Rub the peel around the rim of the glass, then drop it into the drink.

Blending

Used for frozen cocktails, blending combines ingredients with ice to create a smooth, slushy texture. It's perfect for drinks like margaritas or piña coladas.

Ignite

Igniting cocktails adds drama and flavor. Overproof spirits like rum float on top due to their high density. Layer carefully with a spoon, then ignite it safely, keeping hands and flammable materials clear. Always extinguish flames before drinking.

For an alternative, sparklers add excitement without open flames. Use food-safe, slow-burning ones, securing them away from garnishes. Light them just before serving for a dazzling, festive touch that elevates any cocktail.

A Guide to Glassware

Selecting the right glassware for your cocktails can truly enhance their aesthetic appeal and elevate your mixology skills to the next level. Traditionally, certain cocktails are served in specific glasses; for example, a margarita is served in the aptly named wide-brimmed margarita glass, perfect for rimming with salt. However, there are no strict rules for other drinks, so feel free to experiment and have fun finding creative ways to serve your delicious creations that really help sell the theme.

1. Champagne Flute

This tall tulip-shaped glass is designed to show off the magical bubbles of the wine as they burst against the glass. They are great for any cocktail made with sparkling wine.

2. Collins

These tall and narrow glasses originally get their name from collins gin drinks but are now commonly used for a vast array of mixed drinks.

3. Copper Mug

Known for serving the classic Moscow mule, the copper mug is not just visually striking but also helps keep drinks chilled. Its metallic finish adds a stylish flair, making it a favorite for trendy cocktail presentations.

4. Coupe

This saucer-shaped stemmed glass, rumored to have been originally designed after the shape of Marie Antoinette's breast, is traditionally used for serving champagne. However, the wide mouth is not great for containing bubbles and is now more commonly used for cocktails without ice.

5. Highball Glass

Similar to the collins glass but slightly shorter, the highball glass is versatile and ideal for mixed drinks like the classic gin and tonic or whiskey highball. Its straight sides make it easy to hold and sip from.

6. Hurricane Glass

A tall, elegantly cut glass named after its hurricane-lamp-like shape, used for both exotic and tropical drinks.

7. Jam Jar/Mason Jar

Increasingly popular for casual gatherings, the jam jar adds rustic charm to summer parties and barbecues. It's great for serving casual drinks like mojitos, iced teas, or fruity punches, giving a laid-back, homey vibe.

8. Margarita Glass

This glass was designed with one drink in mind. The distinctive double-bowl shape works particularly well for frozen margaritas. The wide rim makes it easy to dress with salt or sugar.

9. Martini

As the name might suggest, this glass was designed for a particular cocktail. These triangle-bowl long-stem glasses are used for a wide range of straight-up (without ice) cocktails.

10. Pitcher

A must-have for any party, a pitcher is perfect for batching cocktails. It allows you to mix and serve drinks easily, making it ideal for gatherings where guests can help themselves to a refreshing pour.

11. Punch Bowl

A punch bowl is essential for serving large quantities of punch at parties. It allows guests to serve themselves and is perfect for festive occasions. For Halloween parties, consider using a cauldron to add a spooky touch to your punch presentation.

12. Rocks Glass

This old-fashioned glass is a short tumbler with a wide base and top, typically associated with whiskey cocktails. The glass was designed to withstand muddling and hold large cubes of ice.

13. Shot Glass

Used for "shooting" a drink, these small glasses are used for a straight pour of a spirit.

14. Stein or Tankard

Steins and tankards are sturdy, often larger mugs typically made from metal, ceramic, or glass, featuring a handle and a lid in some designs. Traditionally associated with German beer culture, they are used primarily for serving beer or hearty cocktails.

15. Tiki Glass

Often elaborately decorated, tiki glasses are perfect for serving exotic, tropical cocktails like mai tais or zombies. Their playful designs add a festive touch to any gathering.

16. Tumbler Glass

A tumbler is a versatile, sturdy glass with a wide bowl and heavy base, perfect for serving cocktails on the rocks, like an old-fashioned or Negroni. Its simple design makes it a go-to choice for both casual and formal settings.

17. Wine Glass

Wine glasses are not just for wine but are used in wine-based cocktails too.

BARTENDER TIP: Chilling glassware before serving a cocktail not only helps maintain the right temperature of the drink but enhances the overall drinking experience.

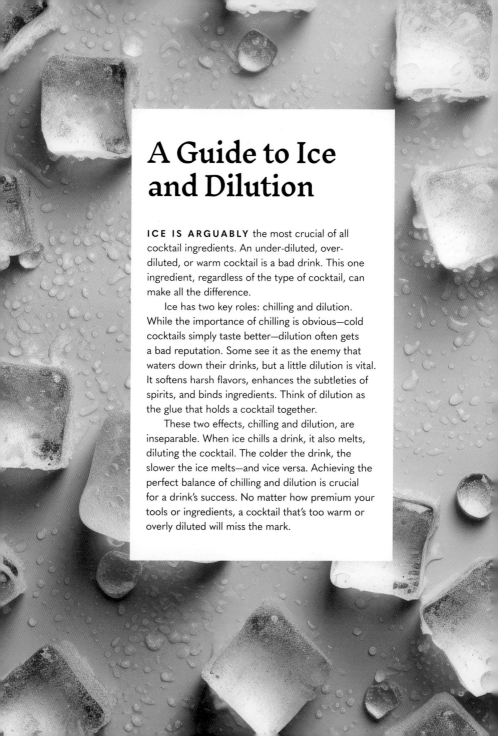

A Guide to Ice and Dilution

ICE IS ARGUABLY the most crucial of all cocktail ingredients. An under-diluted, over-diluted, or warm cocktail is a bad drink. This one ingredient, regardless of the type of cocktail, can make all the difference.

Ice has two key roles: chilling and dilution. While the importance of chilling is obvious—cold cocktails simply taste better—dilution often gets a bad reputation. Some see it as the enemy that waters down their drinks, but a little dilution is vital. It softens harsh flavors, enhances the subtleties of spirits, and binds ingredients. Think of dilution as the glue that holds a cocktail together.

These two effects, chilling and dilution, are inseparable. When ice chills a drink, it also melts, diluting the cocktail. The colder the drink, the slower the ice melts—and vice versa. Achieving the perfect balance of chilling and dilution is crucial for a drink's success. No matter how premium your tools or ingredients, a cocktail that's too warm or overly diluted will miss the mark.

Types of Ice

Block Ice

This type of ice comes in large, solid blocks that are ideal for both mixing and serving cocktails. Block ice melts very slowly, which makes it great for cocktails where you want extended chilling without excessive dilution. Bartenders often use block ice in cocktails served on the rocks to keep them cold without watering them down too quickly. If you want a drink that maintains its integrity over time, block ice is your best friend.

Shard Ice

Shard ice is created when a large piece of ice is broken into irregular fragments. It's used less frequently than other types of ice but is great for both visual appeal and function. The shards melt at a moderate rate, providing quick chilling with controlled dilution. This is a good option for drinks served straight up (without ice in the glass) after they've been shaken or stirred.

Cubed Ice

Standard cubed ice is the workhorse of the cocktail world. Cubes are typically about one inch in diameter and used for most shaking and stirring tasks. They provide an excellent balance of chilling and dilution, making them ideal for mixing a wide variety of drinks. In a glass, they melt at a steady pace, keeping your drink cold without overwhelming dilution. Cubed ice is what you're likely to encounter in most cocktail bars, whether in a chilled glass or when mixing a cocktail.

BARTENDER TIP: To get clear ice cubes at home, use filtered or distilled water and boil it before freezing. Boiling removes air bubbles and impurities that cause cloudiness.

Crushed Ice

When crushed ice is called for, it's because quick chilling and dilution are essential to the cocktail's flavor. This type of ice is perfect for drinks that benefit from an icy, slushy texture—like a mint julep or tiki-style cocktails.

Serving Cocktails with Ice

On the Rocks: A drink served on the rocks is poured over large ice cubes, which melt slowly, keeping the drink colder longer. This is important for spirit-forward drinks like an old-fashioned or whiskey, as it helps preserve flavor without over-diluting.

Straight Up: A straight-up drink is chilled with ice, strained, and served without ice in the glass. This is common for martinis or Manhattans, where the drink is shaken or stirred, then strained into a chilled glass.

Chilled Glass: Chilling the glass helps maintain the drink's temperature. Fill the glass with cubed ice or store it in the freezer before serving to keep the drink as cold as possible. This ensures the drink stays cold while it's being enjoyed.

The Six Major Spirits

The six major spirits—vodka, gin, rum, whiskey, tequila, and brandy—are the basics of any mixologist's cocktail cabinet. These essential spirits serve as the foundation for a wide range of cocktails, offering endless possibilities for creativity. While each spirit has its own character, the beauty of cocktail making lies in your ability to tailor drinks to your taste. Whether you prefer something light and refreshing or bold and complex, these versatile spirits allow you to craft cocktails that suit your style and the occasion.

Vodka

Vodka, known for its neutrality, is distilled from grains or potatoes, offering a clean canvas for cocktails. Flavored vodkas, infused with fruits, herbs, or spices, retain their dry nature unless sweetened. Vodka's versatility makes it a staple in many classic and contemporary cocktails.

Types: plain, flavored, infused

Cocktails Known for:
martini, Moscow mule, Bloody Mary, screwdriver, cosmopolitan

Gin

Gin derives its signature flavor from juniper berries, often accompanied by botanicals like citrus, coriander, and lavender. Styles range from dry London gin to sweeter Old Tom gin. The variety of botanicals used in gin production results in a wide array of flavor profiles, making gin a favorite among bartenders for its versatility.

Types: London dry, Old Tom, Plymouth, genever, sloe gin

Cocktails Known for:
gin and tonic, martini, Greyhound, Tom Collins, French 75, Negroni

Whiskey

Whiskey is a broad category that includes bourbon, Scotch, rye, and Irish whiskey, each defined by its grain, distillation, and aging process. Bourbon is sweet and rich, while Scotch often boasts smoky notes from peat. The aging process in wooden barrels imparts complex flavors and aromas, making whiskey a beloved spirit for sipping and mixing.

Types: Bourbon, Scotch, Irish whiskey, rye, Tennessee whiskey, Canadian whiskey

Cocktails Known for:
Old-Fashioned, whiskey sour, Manhattan, mint julep, boulevardier

BARTENDER TIP: The main difference between liqueurs and liquors is their alcohol content and composition. Liqueurs have a lower alcohol content and add sweetness and complexity to cocktails, while liquors have a higher alcohol content and serve as the base.

Rum

Rum is distilled from sugarcane or molasses, with styles including light, dark, spiced, and overproof. Each type of rum offers distinct flavors, from the light and crisp notes of white rum to the deep, rich flavors of dark rum. Spiced rums add an extra layer of complexity with the addition of spices like cinnamon and vanilla.

Types: light rum (white or silver), dark rum, golden rum, spiced rum, coconut rum, overproof rum, cachaça

Cocktails Known for: mojito, daiquiri, piña colada, Dark and Stormy, mai tai

Tequila

Tequila is made from blue agave, with flavor varying by aging. Blanco tequila is unaged and has a bright, agave-forward flavor, while reposado and añejo tequilas are aged in oak barrels, developing smoother, more complex profiles. Extra añejo tequilas are aged even longer, resulting in a rich, sophisticated spirit.

Types: blanco (light, white, silver), reposado (medium), añejo (dark), extra añejo, joven

Cocktails Known for: margarita, tequila sunrise, paloma, ranch water, El Diablo

Brandy

Brandy is distilled from fermented fruit juice, often grapes, and includes cognac and Armagnac. Aged in barrels, brandy develops warm, fruity, and oaky flavors. Brandy can also be made from other fruits, such as apples (calvados) or pears, offering a diverse range of flavors and aromas.

Types: cognac, Armagnac, pisco, calvados, fruit brandy

Cocktails Known for: sidecar, Brandy Alexander, hot toddy, stinger, Vieux Carré

Celebratory Toasts

Toasting is an ancient tradition that transcends borders and languages. It's a way to express goodwill, celebrate milestones, and bring people together. Whether you're raising a glass at a lively Cinco de Mayo fiesta, honoring tradition at a bar or bat mitzvah, or enjoying a refreshing cocktail by the sun-drenched shores of the South of France, knowing the right toast can elevate any occasion. Here we delve into the rich tapestry of toasting traditions and drinking proverbs from across the globe, ensuring you'll always have the perfect phrase on the tip of your tongue.

Cheers!
(ENGLISH-SPEAKING COUNTRIES)

A universal toast in English-speaking nations, used to express good wishes before drinking.

Sláinte!
(IRELAND)

Meaning "health," this is a common toast, often accompanied by a raised glass.

Prost!
(GERMANY)

A traditional toast meaning "cheers," often used at beer gatherings such as Oktoberfest.

Kanpai!
(JAPAN)

Meaning "empty the glass," this toast is common in Japan, especially at *nomikai* parties which are drinking parties with co-workers.

Banzai!
(JAPAN)

A celebratory toast often used during festive occasions, meaning "ten thousand years."

L'chaim!
(HEBREW)

Meaning "to life," this toast is often used in Jewish celebrations and gatherings.

Salud!
(SPAIN AND LATIN AMERICA)

Meaning "health," this is a popular toast in Spanish-speaking countries.

Cin cin!
(ITALY)

"Cin cin" is believed to have originated from the Chinese "chinchin," meaning "to drink." This phrase has evolved into a joyful expression that resonates throughout Italian culture. Before a toast, it's common to make eye contact with everyone at the table, symbolizing trust and connection. Italians believe that failing to make eye contact during a toast may bring bad luck.

Na zdrowie!
(POLAND)

A toast used in Poland, similar in meaning to "to your health," often accompanied by a shot of vodka.

Skål!
(SCANDINAVIA)

A toast used in Scandinavian countries, meaning "bowl," often referring to a drinking vessel.

À votre santé!
(FRANCE)

Meaning "to your health," this toast is used during meals and celebrations in France.

Santé!
(FRANCE)

Another common toast in France, similar to "cheers."

Origin of the Word "Toast"

The word "toast" originates from the Latin *tostare*, meaning "to roast" or "to brown." Initially, it referred to the practice of adding toasted bread to a drink to enhance its flavor. Over time, this evolved into the custom of raising a glass in honor of someone or something, shifting the meaning from the bread itself to the spoken acknowledgment of celebration.

A Guide to Garnishes

Garnishes can make a cocktail look so gorgeous that you won't be able to stop yourself from flaunting your creations all over social media. However, the significance of a garnish extends far beyond its aesthetic charm; the aroma and flavor it imparts can elevate a cocktail to new heights.

Citrus

Citrus garnishes add a refreshing brightness to any cocktail, elevating its flavor profile with a burst of acidity. Whether it's a classic twist of lemon adorning a gin and tonic, or a vibrant wedge of lime perched atop a margarita, citrus garnishes are the stars of the show.

BARTENDER TIP: For a citrus wheel garnish, use a sharp knife or mandoline to cut thin and even slices, about ⅛ inch (3 mm) thick. For a more elegant presentation and enhanced flavor infusion, lightly dehydrate the wheel.

Edible Glitter

When it comes to edible glitter, the rule is simple: always add sparkle! Edible glitter is a must-have for any girls' night cocktail party, effortlessly transforming drinks into dazzling spectacles. Simply sprinkle a pinch of glitter over the finished drink or rim the glass with a shimmering coat for an extra touch of sparkle. Edible glitters are widely available in a range of colors, and there is always a reason and a season for a little extra.

Edible Flowers

Flowers bring a fresh botanical touch to many cocktails (as well as making drinks super Instagramable) and can be purchased at certain grocery stores or cake decorating supply stores. Commonly used edible flowers in cocktail making include cornflowers, nasturtium, pansies, lavender, orchids, dandelions, and violets, to name a few.

Fruit

Fresh fruits like berries and tropical fruits not only add vibrant colors and visual appeal to your drinks but infuse them with a burst of natural sweetness, acidity, or aromatic oils. Whether you're

garnishing a sophisticated martini with a delicate cherry or adding tropical flair to a rum-based cocktail with a slice of pineapple or a wedge of mango, the right fruit garnish can transform a good cocktail into an exceptional one.

Herbs

Herb garnishes are often used in cocktail making. The herb most frequently used in this book is mint, as it not only looks pretty but adds a sweet refreshing aroma, too. To get the most out of mint, always place the leaves flat between your palms and clap to release their essential oils. Other herbs commonly used are thyme and basil.

Ice Cubes

Infused ice cubes are a delightful way to elevate your cocktails, adding both visual appeal and subtle flavor enhancements. By freezing fruit, flowers, or herbs in ice cube trays, you create stunning, colorful ice that not only keeps your drink chilled but also gradually infuses it with refreshing notes.

Savory Garnishes

A few of the cocktails in this book call for savory garnishes like celery and

olives. This is possibly one of the best ways to add to your daily recommended serving of veggies!

Inedible Flourish

An inedible garnish can play a starring role in bringing your cinematic cocktails to life. These playful and thematic garnishes look fabulous and add a fun, whimsical touch to your cocktail creations. Embrace the tropical holiday vibes with cocktail umbrellas or add some "wow" with an indoor sparkler. The possibilities are endless, so unleash your creativity and let your imagination run wild!

Flavoring Ingredients

Bitters

Bitters are concentrated alcoholic beverages infused with herbs, roots, and fruits, used to add depth and complexity to cocktails. They serve as flavor enhancers and aromatic agents, added in small quantities due to their intense flavor. Some commonly used bitters include brands such as Angostura, known for its spicy and aromatic profile, and Peychaud's, which offers a lighter, anise-flavored touch; and orange bitters, which add a citrusy zest. These bitters are essential for creating well-balanced and flavorful cocktails.

BARTENDER TIP: These concentrated flavorings can add depth and complexity to your cocktails. Use them sparingly to enhance the drink.

Butterfly Pea Flower

Available online (we recommend brands such as b'Lure flower extract) or in certain kitchenware stores, this relatively unknown ingredient will turn drinks from blue to purple, and then pink with only a few drops! Used throughout Asia in traditional medicine and as a food coloring, this unique ingredient acts as a kind of litmus, changing color with the acidity of a drink.

Citrus Juices

Lemon, lime, or grapefruit juice can be found in most cocktails. These ingredients offer an acidic element that counterbalances sweetness to give a cocktail a well-balanced flavor profile. It is always preferable to use freshly squeezed citrus juice when making a cocktail.

Eggs

Several cocktails in this book incorporate egg whites to enhance viscosity and create a frothy foam by trapping air bubbles. However, if you are vegan, aquafaba (the water used to cook beans, such as chickpeas) can be used as a substitute for egg whites.

Liqueurs

Liqueurs are sweetened spirits infused with flavors from fruits, herbs, spices, nuts and even chocolate. These versatile ingredients add depth, complexity, and a touch of sweetness to cocktails, enhancing both flavor and texture. Liqueurs can range from light and fruity to rich and creamy. Whether used as the primary ingredient or as a subtle accent, liqueurs play a crucial role in creating balanced, innovative drinks, making them an essential component in any cocktail collection.

Triple sec (orange-flavored): Adds citrus brightness to margaritas and sidecars.

Amaretto (almond-flavored): Sweet and nutty, perfect for amaretto sours.

Coffee liqueur: Adds depth to White Russians and espresso martinis.

Herbal liqueurs: Chartreuse and Bénédictine provide unique herbal flavors.

Syrups

Custom cocktail syrups are one of those special ingredients that can magically transform a drink. Whether it's simple syrup or a seasonal flavor combination—such as gingerbread syrup for winter or a bright, fruity passion fruit syrup for summer—these versatile creations elevate any cocktail. Best of all, they are easy to prepare at home, allowing bartenders and enthusiasts alike to tailor flavors to perfectly suit any theme. When working with heated sugar, it's important to handle it carefully to avoid burns, and syrups should be stored properly to maintain quality. Below are some of the cocktail syrups featured in this book. These recipes serve as a starting point for crafting signature flavors.

Bartender Tip: Once made, syrups can be stored in the refrigerator for up to one month.

Simple Syrup

Sometimes referred to as sugar syrup, this essential cocktail staple is a supersaturated mixture of sugar and water. The most common recipe uses two parts sugar to one part water (2:1).

1 cup (200 g) sugar
½ cup (120 ml) water

1. Combine sugar and water in a small saucepan over medium heat.
2. Stir until the sugar is fully dissolved.
3. Remove from heat and allow the syrup to cool completely.
4. Store in a clean glass bottle or jar in the refrigerator.

Gingerbread Syrup

This warmly spiced syrup is perfect for holiday cocktails, adding cozy flavors of cinnamon, clove, and molasses.

½ cup (100 g) sugar
½ cup (120 ml) water
1 tablespoon (12 g) dark brown sugar
1 tablespoon (20 g) molasses
1 tablespoon (7 g) ground cinnamon
½ teaspoon ground cloves

1. In a small saucepan, combine water, sugars, molasses, cinnamon, and cloves.
2. Bring to a simmer over medium heat, stirring occasionally until the sugar is dissolved.
3. Reduce heat and simmer gently for 10 to 15 minutes.
4. Remove from heat and let the syrup cool slightly.
5. Strain through a fine-mesh sieve into a clean container, discarding solids.
6. Allow to cool completely before storing in a glass bottle or jar.

Honey syrup

Also known as liquid honey, this syrup adds a floral sweetness to cocktails and is an effortless way to incorporate honey into drinks.

½ cup (170 g) honey

½ cup (120 ml) water

1. Combine honey and water in a small saucepan.

2. Heat over low heat, stirring until dissolved (about 1 minute).

3. Let the syrup cool, then strain into a jar or bottle.

4. Seal tightly and refrigerate.

BARTENDER TIP: Use honey syrup in cocktails featuring tea or citrus to enhance its natural floral notes.

Elderflower Syrup

This floral syrup adds a touch of sweetness to a cocktail, perfect for springtime drinks when a fragrant bloom is in the air.

½ cup (about 10 to 12 flower heads) fresh elderflowers

2 cups (475 ml) water

1 cup (200 g) granulated sugar

½ lemon, sliced

1. Gently rinse the elderflower heads under cold water and set aside to drain.

2. In a medium saucepan, combine the water, sugar, and lemon slices. Heat over medium heat, stirring until the sugar is fully dissolved.

3. Once the sugar has dissolved, bring the mixture to a gentle boil. Remove from heat and add the elderflowers. Stir gently to combine.

4. Cover the saucepan and allow the elderflower mixture to steep for 24 hours at room temperature to develop the flavor.

5. After steeping, strain the mixture through a fine-mesh sieve, pressing on the solids to extract as much liquid as possible. Discard the solids.

6. Pour the syrup into clean bottles or jars. Seal tightly and store in the refrigerator.

Lavender and Rose Syrup

This fragrant floral syrup adds a delicate sweetness to cocktails, with the soothing essence of lavender and a hint of rose.

⅛ cup (about 2 to 3 tablespoons) dried lavender flowers

2 cups (475 ml) water

1 cup (200 g) granulated sugar

½ lemon, sliced

A dash of rose water

1. Gently rinse the lavender flowers under cold water, then set aside to drain.

2. In a medium saucepan, combine the water, sugar, and lemon slices. Heat over medium heat, stirring until the sugar fully dissolves.

3. Once the sugar has dissolved, bring the mixture to a gentle boil. Remove from heat and stir in the lavender flowers.

4. Cover the saucepan and let the mixture steep for 24 hours at room temperature to infuse the flavors.

5. After steeping, strain the mixture through a fine-mesh sieve, pressing gently to extract as much liquid as possible. Discard the solids.

6. Stir in a dash of rose water, then pour the syrup into clean bottles or jars. Seal tightly and store in the refrigerator.

Raspberry Syrup

This vibrant syrup is a fruity addition to summer cocktails and spritzers.

⅓ pound (150 g) fresh raspberries

½ cup (120 ml) water

⅓ cup (67 g) sugar

1. Add raspberries, water, and sugar to a small saucepan.

2. Heat over medium heat, stirring until the sugar dissolves.

3. Bring to a gentle boil, then reduce heat and simmer for 10 to 15 minutes, until the raspberries soften.

4. Remove from heat and let cool slightly.

5. Strain through a fine-mesh sieve, pressing on the solids to extract as much liquid as possible.

6. Discard solids and transfer the syrup to a clean bottle or jar. Let cool completely before storing.

Marshmallow Syrup

This syrup is perfect for adding a sweet, creamy touch to your cocktails.

½ cup (118 ml) mini marshmallows (or 10 to 12 large marshmallows)

½ cup (120 ml) water

¼ cup (50 g) granulated sugar

1 teaspoon vanilla extract

1. Combine marshmallows, water, and sugar in a small saucepan.

2. Heat over medium heat, stirring constantly, until the marshmallows are melted, and the sugar is fully dissolved (about 2 to 3 minutes).

3. Remove from heat and stir in the vanilla extract.

4. For a smoother syrup, strain the mixture through a fine mesh sieve to remove any undissolved marshmallow bits.

5. Let the syrup cool, then strain into a jar or bottle if needed.

6. Seal tightly and refrigerate.

Passion Fruit Syrup

Tart and tropical, this syrup adds a burst of exotic flavor to cocktails.

½ cup (100 g) sugar

½ cup (120 ml) water

4 ripe passion fruits

1. Combine sugar and water in a small saucepan over low heat, stirring occasionally until the sugar dissolves.

2. Remove from heat and slice the passion fruits in half.

3. Scoop the pulp into the simple syrup and let steep for 2 hours.

4. Strain through a fine-mesh sieve, allowing the syrup to drain naturally without pressing the solids.

5. Discard solids and transfer the syrup to a clean glass bottle or jar. Let cool completely before refrigerating.

BARTENDER TIP: Use passion fruit syrup in tiki-inspired cocktails to add a tropical flair.

Winter
CHEERS & COZY CELEBRATIONS

THIS CHAPTER IS DEDICATED TO cocktails that capture the essence of the celebrations that fill the early months of the year. Even as the trees stand bare and the days grow shorter, winter offers countless reasons to dress up, enjoy a drink (or two), and catch up with friends, both old and new.

From festive Christmas cocktail parties to dazzling New Year's Eve soirees, cozy Valentine's Day dinners to laid-back après ski gatherings, the winter season is brimming with opportunities to raise a glass with those you love. Whether you're sipping on a warming hot toddy, enjoying a winter fruit-infused martini, or savoring a spiced mulled wine, each drink is a perfect way to make these chilly months feel special.

In this chapter, you will find cocktails bursting with the rich, comforting flavors that define the season. Ingredients like cinnamon, nutmeg, cloves, and ginger evoke memories of Christmas markets and festive fun. Spirits like whiskey, rum, and brandy shine in winter drinks, providing a robust base that pairs well with the sweetness of honey, maple syrup, or dark winter fruits like cranberry and pomegranate.

So, mark your calendar and start sending out those save-the-date reminders: 'Tis the season to celebrate! With cocktails as stunning and delicious as the ones featured here, your party schedule is sure to be full for the next several months.

WINTER WONDERLAND

PREPARATION TIME:
5 minutes

GLASSWARE:
Coupe glass

CELEBRATION:
Christmas

SERVES: 1

Handful of fresh
cranberries

1 ounce (30 ml)
honey syrup
(see recipe on page 41)

1 ounce (30 ml)
fresh lime juice

1 ounce (30 ml)
cranberry juice

2 ounces (60 ml)
silver tequila

Ice cubes

GARNISH:
Granulated sugar,
cranberries, and
a rosemary sprig

GET READY TO COZY UP with a cocktail that feels like a snow day in a glass! This shimmering, frost-kissed drink is perfect for soaking in the magic of the season. Whether you're watching the first snowflakes fall from the comfort of your couch or hosting a festive holiday get-together, this cocktail is a total crowd-pleaser with its gorgeous wintry vibes and delicious flavors.

The Winter Wonderland cocktail brings together the tart zing of fresh cranberries, the smooth sweetness of honey syrup, and the bold, cozy warmth of tequila. It's perfectly balanced, super tasty, and guaranteed to transport you to a dreamy and snowy escape with every sip.

Add an extra sprinkle of winter magic by garnishing the cocktail with cranberries rolled in granulated sugar, transforming them into frosted gems that sparkle as if touched by Jack Frost himself.

1. *Start by preparing the honey syrup (see recipe on page 41).*

2. *In the can of the cocktail shaker muddle the cranberries and the honey syrup together.*

3. *Combine the fresh lime juice, cranberry juice and silver tequila in the cocktail shaker with a handful of ice cubes. Shake until the mixture is cool.*

4. *Strain the cocktail into a chilled martini coupe glass.*

5. *To garnish, dip the cranberries and rosemary sprig into some honey syrup. Then place some granulated sugar into a small bowl and dip the moistened cranberries and rosemary sprig into the sugar. Set them aside to dry before decorating the cocktail.*

6. *Spear three frosted cranberries with a cocktail stick and balance the rosemary sprig on the rim of the glass.*

GINGERBREAD MARTINI

EMBRACE THE FESTIVE SPIRIT of the season with the Gingerbread Martini, a cocktail that transforms everyone's favorite holiday treat into a delightful drink. This irresistible mix of smooth vodka, spiced ginger syrup, and rich coffee liqueur perfectly captures the warm and cozy flavors of freshly baked gingerbread cookies with every sip.

To elevate the experience, you can even bake your own gingerbread cookie garnishes, which can be artfully perched on the rim of your glass. Invite friends and family to decorate their own gingerbread creations, adding a unique and personal flair to every cocktail.

Whether you're decking the halls, wrapping presents, or simply basking in the glow of twinkling lights, this delicious duo of cocktail and cookie is the perfect way to sip, snack, and celebrate the season with style and cheer.

1. *Rim a martini glass (learn how to rim a glass on page 19) with the crushed gingerbread crumbs and maple syrup.*

2. *Combine the vodka, gingerbread syrup (see recipe on page 40), heavy cream, and coffee liqueur into a cocktail shaker with a handful of ice cubes and shake vigorously until the mixture is cool.*

3. *Carefully strain the cocktail into the prepared gingerbread-rimmed martini glass and garnish with a gingerbread cookie, a flourish of whipped cream, and a dusting of cinnamon.*

PREPARATION TIME:
15 to 30 minutes

GLASSWARE:
Martini glass

CELEBRATION:
Christmas

SERVES: 1

2 ounces (60 ml) vodka

1 ounce (30 ml) gingerbread syrup (see recipe on page 40)

1 ounce (30 ml) heavy cream

½ ounce (15 ml) coffee liqueur

Ice cubes

GARNISH:
1 tablespoon (20 g) of maple syrup for decorating the glass, gingerbread crumbs (for rimming the glass), gingerbread cookie, whipped cream, cinnamon

MERRY NOG-MAS

PREPARATION TIME:
2 to 3 hours

GLASSWARE:
Martini glass

CELEBRATION:
Christmas

SERVES: 4

4 eggs

½ cup (100 g) sugar

2 cups (475 ml) whole milk

1 cup (235 ml) heavy cream

½ teaspoon nutmeg

½ teaspoon vanilla extract

¼ teaspoon ground cinnamon

3 ounces (90 ml) bourbon

3 ounces (90 ml) amaretto/almond-flavored liqueur

GARNISH:
Whipped cream, cinnamon stick, nutmeg

CELEBRATE THE FESTIVE SEASON with the Merry Nog-mas cocktail, a delightful twist on the classic eggnog that will warm your spirits and add cheer to your holiday gatherings! This creamy concoction combines rich eggnog with spiced rum, a splash of vanilla, and a hint of nutmeg, creating a luscious drink that embodies the cozy essence of Christmas.

Its smooth, velvety texture and comforting flavors make it a must-have addition to your holiday celebrations.

1. *In a medium bowl, whisk the eggs and sugar together until the mixture is smooth and slightly thickened.*

2. *In a saucepan, combine the whole milk and heavy cream. Heat over medium heat until warm but not boiling. Stir occasionally.*

3. *Slowly add a small amount of the warm milk-and-cream mixture to the egg-and-sugar mixture, whisking constantly to prevent the eggs from cooking.*

4. *Gradually add the rest of the warm milk-and-cream mixture to the eggs, whisking until well combined.*

5. *Pour the mixture back into the saucepan and cook over low to medium heat, stirring constantly, until the mixture thickens slightly (about 5 to 7 minutes). Do not let it boil.*

6. *Once thickened, remove from heat and stir in the nutmeg, vanilla extract, and cinnamon (if using).*

7. *Allow the eggnog to cool to room temperature, then refrigerate for at least 2 hours to chill.*

8. *Before serving, add the bourbon and the almond-flavored liqueur to the eggnog and whisk lightly to incorporate any separation.*

9. *Top each glass with a dollop of whipped cream and a sprinkle of nutmeg for extra flavor and festive flair.*

WINTER MEDAL MULE

RAISE YOUR GLASS TO VICTORY with the Winter Medal Mule, a cocktail that captures the excitement and camaraderie of the Winter Olympics. This refreshing twist on the classic Moscow Mule features a bold blend of ginger, lime, and vodka, served in a gleaming copper mug—a true champion's vessel.

The icy chill of the copper mug keeps your drink perfectly crisp, making it the ultimate refreshment as you cheer on your favorite athletes in thrilling events like bobsleigh, curling, and ice hockey. With every sip, feel the spirit of the Games come alive, as if you're standing on the podium, basking in the glory of victory.

Whether you're hosting a watch party or simply soaking in the festive energy of the Winter Olympics, the Winter Medal Mule is a true celebration of competition, camaraderie, and winter sports. Just like all the athletes striving for gold, this drink is a winner in its own right.

1. *Into a copper mug, lightly muddle the mint leaves, vodka, and fresh lime juice.*

2. *Next, pack the glass tightly with crushed ice. Stir until the cup is frosted on the outside.*

3. *Top with chilled ginger beer and gently stir to combine the ingredients.*

4. *Garnish with a lime wedge and a sprig of fresh mint.*

PREPARATION TIME:
5 minutes

GLASSWARE:
Copper mug

CELEBRATION:
Winter Olympics

SERVES: 1

8 mint leaves

2 ounces (60 ml) vodka

½ ounce (15 ml) fresh lime juice

4 ounces (120 ml) ginger beer

Crushed ice

GARNISH:
Lime wedge and mint sprig

SPARKLING CELEBRATION

WELCOME THE NEW YEAR with a touch of glamour and sophistication as you sip the Sparkling Celebration cocktail—a dazzling twist on the classic French 75. This elegant blend of champagne and elderflower liqueur delivers a light, refreshing flavor that embodies the spirit of festivity, making it the perfect choice for your New Year's Eve soirée.

Served in delicate champagne flutes and adorned with edible glitter, this cocktail is as enchanting as the occasion itself. For an added flourish, top each glass with a shimmering sparkler, creating a stunning display that's sure to captivate your guests and set the mood for the countdown.

As the clock strikes midnight and the familiar strains of "Auld Lang Syne" fill the air, raise your glass in a joyful toast to new beginnings. With its effervescent charm and celebratory sparkle, the Sparkling Celebration cocktail is the perfect companion for clinking flutes, cherishing memories, and welcoming the year ahead with style.

1. *Into a chilled champagne flute combine the elderflower liqueur and edible gold glitter.*

2. *Gently pour the champagne or sparkling wine into the glass.*

3. *Garnish with a lemon twist and a dusting of edible gold leaf for that extra glamorous touch. For the final flourish, place a miniature sparkler in the glass, and light before serving. Remove and safely dispose of the spent sparkler before drinking!*

PREPARATION TIME:
5 minutes

GLASSWARE:
Champagne flute

CELEBRATION:
New Year's Eve

SERVES: 1

½ ounce (15 ml) elderflower liqueur

Pinch of edible gold glitter

Champagne (or sparkling wine)

GARNISH:
Lemon twist, dusting of edible gold leaf, and miniature sparkler

LUNAR MARTINI

PREPARATION TIME:
5 minutes

GLASSWARE:
Martini glass

CELEBRATION:
Chinese New Year

SERVES: 1

1½ ounces (45 ml) vodka

1 ounce (30 ml)
lychee liqueur

½ ounce (15 ml)
fresh lime juice

½ ounce (15 ml)
simple syrup
(see recipe on page 40)

Pinch of edible
gold glitter

Ice cubes

GARNISH:
Fresh lychee fruit rolled
in edible gold glitter
on a cocktail stick

THE LUNAR NEW YEAR IS A TREASURED
celebration across many Asian cultures, symbolizing
renewal, prosperity, and the promise of a fresh start.
Marked by the second new moon after the winter
solstice, this vibrant festival comes alive with dazzling
fireworks, lively parades featuring lion and dragon
dancers, and the cherished tradition of gifting red
envelopes—symbols of good fortune. Central to the
festivities are the color red, which represents luck and
joy, and citrus fruits like oranges and limes, believed to
usher in abundance and positivity.

Inspired by these meaningful traditions, the
Lunar Martini is a toast to the spirit of the season.
This elegant cocktail combines the delicate sweetness
of lychee with the bright, refreshing zest of citrus,
creating a harmonious blend that captures the essence
of celebration. With its vibrant flavors and symbolic
ingredients, the Lunar Martini is the perfect way to honor
the traditions of the Lunar New Year while welcoming a
prosperous year ahead.

1. *Combine the vodka, lychee liqueur, lime juice,
   simple syrup (see recipe on page 40), and a pinch
   of edible gold glitter into a cocktail shaker along
   with a handful of ice cubes. Shake vigorously
   until the mixture is cool.*

2. *Carefully strain the mixture into a chilled martini
   glass. Garnish with a peeled lychee fruit rolled in
   edible gold glitter on a cocktail stick.*

VODKA-SOAKED VALENTINE'S

FALL HEAD OVER HEELS for the Vodka-Soaked Valentine's martini, a decadent creation that is as sweet and irresistible as love itself. This indulgent blend of fresh strawberries, vanilla vodka, rich Irish cream liqueur, and scoops of velvety ice cream is the ultimate way to celebrate romance with a dessert that has a delightful boozy twist.

Crowned with fluffy whipped cream and a scattering of candy heart sprinkles, this cocktail is a love letter in liquid form. Perfect for setting the stage for an intimate dinner for two or adding a touch of romance to a Valentine's Day party, the Vodka-Soaked Valentine's martini is your invitation to celebrate the season of love in the most delicious way.

1. *In a blender combine the strawberries, coffee liqueur, vanilla vodka, Irish cream liqueur, and ice cream. Blend until smooth.*

2. *Strain the mixture into two glasses and garnish with whipped cream, a sprinkling of sugar hearts, and a raspberry on a cocktail stick.*

PREPARATION TIME:
5 minutes

GLASSWARE:
Ice cream glass

CELEBRATION:
Valentine's Day

SERVES: 2

10 strawberries, hulled

2 ounces (60 ml) coffee liqueur

2 ounces (60 ml) vanilla vodka

2 ounces (60 ml) Irish cream liqueur

2 scoops vanilla ice cream

Ice cubes

GARNISH:
Whipped cream, sugar hearts, and a fresh raspberry

THE SCARLET STAR

PREPARATION TIME:
10 minutes

GLASSWARE:
Coupe glass

CELEBRATION:
Awards shows

SERVES: 1

⅘ ounce (24 ml)
raspberry syrup
(see recipe on page 42)

1¾ ounces (52 ml) gin

⅘ ounce (24 ml)
fresh lemon juice

½ ounce (15 ml)
egg white

Ice cubes

GARNISH:
Three fresh raspberries
on a cocktail stick and a
dusting of edible gold leaf

STEP INTO THE SPOTLIGHT with The Scarlet Star, a signature cocktail that could be crowned Best Cocktail of the Year and is worthy of Hollywood's brightest nights. Just like the stars that grace Tinseltown's biggest awards shows, this drink radiates glamour, elegance, and undeniable allure. Its deep scarlet hue, adorned with a sprinkle of edible gold leaf, captures the opulence of the red carpet, while its bold blend of raspberry syrup, sharp lemon juice, and frothy egg whites delivers a performance that's nothing short of award-winning.

Perfect for an awards-show viewing party or your own night of cinematic celebration, The Scarlet Star is the ultimate toast to fame and fortune. Sip this masterpiece as you bask in the glow of the spotlight, channelling the poise and charm of the evening's biggest stars. With each sip, you'll feel like you've taken home the gold yourself.

1. *Combine the raspberry syrup (see recipe on page 42), gin, lemon juice, and egg white into a cocktail shaker along with a handful of ice cubes. Shake until cold and the egg white is frothy.*

2. *Carefully strain the mixture into a chilled coupe glass.*

3. *Garnish with fresh raspberries a cocktail stick with a dusting of edible gold leaf to guarantee the best-dressed cocktail.*

SHADOW SPRITZ

PREPARATION TIME:
5 minutes + overnight
for ice cubes

GLASSWARE:
Collins glass

CELEBRATION:
Groundhog Day

SERVES: 1

1½ ounces (45 ml)
botanic gin

¾ ounce (20 ml)
elderflower liqueur

½ ounce (15 ml)
fresh lime juice

Ice cubes with
edible violets

Tonic water

GARNISH:
A few extra edible violets

RAISE A GLASS TO THE QUIRKY CHARM of Groundhog Day with the Shadow Spritz, a cocktail that playfully captures the essence of this beloved tradition. Just as the groundhog's shadow foretells the transition from winter to spring, this drink symbolizes the changing seasons.

Simple to create yet stunningly elegant, the ice cube encasing edible violets symbolizes the first blossoms of spring. As it slowly melts, it mirrors the gentle retreat of winter and the approach of brighter, warmer days. Each sip offers a refreshing taste of renewal.

Whether the forecast calls for six more weeks of winter or an early spring, the Shadow Spritz is perfect for drinking on repeat.

TO PREPARE THE FLORAL ICE CUBES:

1. *Boil water and let it cool to room temperature (boiled water cools clearer than tap water).*

2. *Fill an ice cube tray with the cooled boiled water.*

3. *Carefully place a few edible violets in each compartment, making sure they are evenly spaced and submerged.*

4. *Freeze until solid, which may take a few hours.*

TO PREPARE THE COCKTAIL:

5. *Fill a collins glass with the previously prepared floral ice cubes.*

6. *Pour the gin, elderflower liqueur, and fresh lime juice and stir gently to combine.*

7. *Top up with tonic water and garnish with a few extra edible violets for visual appeal.*

IRISH HOPPER

CELEBRATE ST. PATRICK'S DAY in style with the Irish Hopper, a festive twist on the classic grasshopper cocktail that brings the spirit of Ireland right to your glass! This enchanting libation features a luscious blend of Irish cream liqueur, refreshing mint liqueur, and smooth chocolate liqueur, creating a decadent drink that's as rich as the Emerald Isle itself.

With its vibrant green hue, the Irish Hopper is a nod to the shamrocks and leprechauns of St. Patrick's Day, offering a refined alternative to the traditional pint of Guinness. Served chilled and garnished with a sprig of fresh mint, this cocktail is as festive as it is elegant. For an extra touch of Irish luck, top it off with a sprinkle of edible gold. *Sláinte!*

1. *Combine the crème de cacao, crème de menthe, and heavy cream into a cocktail shaker with a handful of ice cubes. Shake until cool.*

2. *Strain the mixture into chilled martini glasses and garnish with a fresh mint sprig, a dusting of grated mint chocolate, and a sprinkle of gold leaf for a touch of Irish luck.*

PREPARATION TIME:
5 minutes

GLASSWARE:
Martini glass

CELEBRATION:
Saint Patrick's Day

SERVES: 1

1 ounce (30 ml)
crème de cacao (white)

1 ounce (30 ml)
crème de menthe (green)

1 ounce (30 ml)
heavy cream

Ice cubes

GARNISH:
Mint spring, mint chocolate crumbs, and gold leaf

MARDI GRAS HURRICANE

PREPARATION TIME:
5 minutes

GLASSWARE:
Hurricane glass

CELEBRATION:
Mardi Gras

SERVES: 1

2 ounces (60 ml)
light rum

2 ounces (60 ml)
dark rum

2 ounces (60 ml)
passion fruit juice

1 ounce (30 ml)
orange juice

½ ounce (15 ml)
fresh lime juice

½ ounce (15 ml)
simple syrup
(see recipe on page 40)

1 teaspoon grenadine syrup

Pinch of edible glitter

Ice cubes

GARNISH:
Orange slice, glacé cherries,
and miniature sparkler

CAPTURE THE VIBRANT SPIRIT OF MARDI GRAS with this Hurricane cocktail, a dazzling drink that embodies the energy and excitement of this legendary festival. Known for its colorful parades, glittering costumes, and electrifying atmosphere, Mardi Gras transforms the streets into a celebration of music, joy, and revelry—and this cocktail is the perfect companion.

Blending smooth rum with tropical passion fruit and orange juices, the splash of grenadine adds a burst of sweetness and a strikingly colorful presentation. Served over ice in a signature hurricane glass and garnished with a juicy orange slice and a bright cherry, it's as festive and eye-catching as the beads and masks that define the season.

Raise your glass and let the Mardi Gras Hurricane whisk you away to the heart of New Orleans. *Laissez les bon temps rouler*—let the good times roll!

1. *Combine the light rum, dark rum, passion fruit juice, orange juice, lime juice, simple syrup (see recipe on page 40), grenadine and glitter into a cocktail shaker with a handful of ice cubes and shake vigorously until the mixture is cool.*

2. *Add ice cubes into the hurricane glass, then carefully strain the cocktail into the glass.*

3. *Add more ice to fill the glass and top up with extra orange juice if needed.*

4. *Garnish with an orange slice and glacé cherries. For the final flourish, secure a miniature sparkler into the orange, and light before serving. Remove and safely dispose of the spent sparkler before drinking!*

SIDELINE SPLASH

GET READY TO SCORE BIG at your game day celebration with the Sideline Splash, a refreshing cocktail that's perfect for the big game! This vibrant punch combines smooth vodka, tropical pineapple juice, zesty blue curaçao, and bubbly lemon-lime soda, delivering a refreshing burst of flavor that's as lively as the action on the field.

Served in a large punch bowl, the Sideline Splash is perfect for game day or tailgating parties, and it can be easily prepped ahead of time and chilled in a cooler—so you can spend less time mixing and more time enjoying the game. Whether you're rooting for your favorite team, catching the halftime show, or just here for the snacks, this colorful cocktail ensures you'll be the MVP.

1. *Fill a pitcher halfway up with ice cubes.*

2. *Add the vodka, blue curaçao, lemon juice, and lemon-lime soda into the pitcher. Stir well with a bar spoon to combine.*

3. *Using a star-shaped cookie cutter, cut pineapple slices into star shapes.*

4. *Serve in cups or plastic stadium cups for the full game-day experience and garnish with a star-shaped pineapple slice.*

PREPARATION TIME:
10 minutes

GLASSWARE:
Large pitcher and cups

CELEBRATION:
Game day!

SERVES: 8+

12 ounces (355 ml) vodka

8 ounces (235 ml) blue curaçao

4 ounces (120 ml) fresh lemon juice

32 ounces (950 ml) lemon-lime soda

Ice cubes

GARNISH:
Lemon slices, orange slices, pineapple slices cut into stars

2

Spring

SIPS & GARDEN GATHERINGS

SPRING IS A SEASON OF RENEWAL, growth, and boundless energy—a time when nature bursts back to life, and the days grow longer with the promise of warmer weather ahead. This chapter celebrates the vibrant spirit of spring with cocktails that reflect the freshness and vitality of the season.

As blossoms fill the air and greenery awakens, it's the perfect time to savor bright, herbal flavors and refreshing ingredients that mirror the world's renewal. Inside, you'll discover indulgent Easter egg–inspired creations, sophisticated drinks for honoring Mother's Day, and lively libations to capture the joy of Carnival.

Spring is more than a season of nature's revival; it's a time to gather with loved ones and toast to life's special moments. Whether you're celebrating new beginnings or simply soaking in the beauty of the season, these cocktails are crafted to elevate your springtime gatherings with their refreshing flavors, festive flair, and seasonal charm.

CARNIVAL CAIPIRINHA

PREPARATION TIME:
5 minutes

GLASSWARE:
Rocks glass

CELEBRATION:
Carnival

SERVES: 1

2 ounces (60 ml)
cachaça (or light rum)

½ ounce (15 ml)
passion fruit juice
(fresh or nectar)

½ ounce (15 ml)
lime juice

½ ounce (15 ml)
passion fruit syrup
(see recipe on page 43)

2 lime wedges

3 to 4 fresh mint leaves

Crushed ice

GARNISH:
Mint sprig, lime wheel,
and edible flower

INFUSED WITH THE ELECTRIFYING ENERGY of Brazilian Carnival, the Carnival Caipirinha brings the celebration straight to your glass. This bold, refreshing twist on Brazil's iconic caipirinha showcases the vibrant flavors of cachaça—a sugarcane-based spirit as dynamic as the samba itself.

Each sip is a celebration, as the smooth cachaça transports you to the heart of the festivities, where music, dancing, and joy fill the air.

Perfect for setting the mood at your own party or enjoying as you sway to the rhythm of samba beats, the Carnival Caipirinha is your ticket to Brazil's most iconic celebration and a splashy way to welcome spring's arrival. Let this vibrant cocktail awaken your inner dancer and ignite an unforgettable night of laughter, music, and revelry. *Saúde!*

1. *In a sturdy rocks glass, add the mint leaves and freshly cut lime wedges. Muddle them together gently to release the oils and juice.*

2. *Pour in the cachaça, passion fruit juice, lime juice, and passion fruit syrup (see recipe on page 43) into the glass.*

3. *Fill the glass with crushed ice and gently stir with a bar spoon to combine.*

4. *Top the cocktail with a fresh mint sprig and a lime wheel. Add an edible flower for an extra splash of color and glamour, giving it that carnival magic.*

BLOSSOM BREEZE

CELEBRATE THE ARRIVAL OF SPRING with the
Blossom Breeze, a cocktail inspired by the delicate,
fleeting beauty of cherry blossoms in full bloom. This
exquisite creation marries the sweet allure of cherry
with the floral elegance of premium gin and a whisper
of elderflower, capturing the essence of a blossoming
garden within a martini glass.

To make this cocktail truly picture-perfect, garnish
with real edible cherry blossom flowers, transforming
each glass into a work of art. The delicate blooms add a
touch of natural beauty, making it an ideal centerpiece
for spring gatherings and an Instagram-worthy toast to
the season.

Light, fragrant, and delightfully refreshing,
the Blossom Breeze is more than just a drink—it's
a celebration of renewal, growth, and the vibrant
possibilities of spring. Gather your friends, bask in the
sunshine, and raise a glass to the magic of the season with
this floral-inspired delight.

1. *Combine the gin, cherry liqueur, elderflower liqueur,
   lemon juice, honey syrup (see recipe on page 41), and
   orange blossom water into a cocktail shaker along
   with a handful of ice cubes. Shake vigorously until
   the mixture is cool.*

2. *Carefully strain the mixture into a chilled martini
   glass. Garnish with a cherry on a cocktail stick and
   float some cherry blossoms on top.*

PREPARATION TIME:
5 minutes

GLASSWARE:
Martini glass

CELEBRATION:
Spring blossoms

SERVES: 1

2 ounces (60 ml) gin

¾ ounce (22 ml)
cherry liqueur

½ ounce (15 ml)
elderflower liqueur

½ ounce (15 ml)
fresh lemon juice

¼ ounce (7.5 ml)
honey syrup
(see recipe on page 41)

2 dashes of orange
blossom water

Ice cubes

GARNISH:
Cherry and edible flowers
(preferably cherry blossoms
petals when in season)

EASTER EGGSTRAVAGANZA

PREPARATION TIME:
5 minutes

GLASSWARE:
Chocolate Easter egg

CELEBRATION:
Easter

SERVES: 1

3 ounces (90 ml)
Irish cream liqueur

6 scoops vanilla
ice cream

1 large hollow
chocolate Easter egg

Ice cubes

GARNISH:
Chocolate sauce,
whipped cream,
chopped nuts, and
mini chocolate eggs

BARTENDER TIP: For an elegant presentation, serve the Easter Eggstravaganza in a meringue nest to support the egg and keep it perfectly balanced.

HOP INTO THE EASTER SPIRIT with the Easter Eggstravaganza, a show-stopping cocktail that's as fun to make as it is to enjoy. Served in a hollow chocolate egg, this decadent creation is a chocoholic's dream come true. A luscious blend of Irish cream liqueur, velvety ice cream, and rich chocolate sauce comes together to create a drink that's pure indulgence in every sip.

The best part of this cocktail is the creative freedom to decorate and garnish it with all your favorite chocolates and candies. Whether it's a swirl of whipped cream, a drizzle of rich chocolate sauce, crunchy nuts, colorful sprinkles, or mini chocolate eggs, your favorite sweet treats can make this cocktail both irresistibly delicious and picture-perfect.

This dessert cocktail is a celebration of all things sweet and indulgent, perfect for those who love life's little luxuries. And when the last drop has been drunk, the best part awaits—your delicious chocolate egg, ready to be devoured! The Easter Eggstravaganza is the ultimate boozy treat to make your Easter celebrations extra special and irresistibly sweet.

1. *Carefully crack off the top of the chocolate Easter egg (and enjoy any stray chocolate bits!).*

2. *Blend the Irish cream liqueur, and ice cream together, until smooth, then pour into the chocolate eggs.*

3. *Top with whipped cream, a drizzle of chocolate sauce, chopped nuts, mini chocolate eggs, and chocolate sprinkles.*

TRICKSTER'S TREAT

CELEBRATE THE PLAYFUL SPIRIT of April Fools' Day with the Trickster's Treat, a mischievous twist on the classic margarita. Inspired by centuries of surprises and fun that occur on April 1st, this tequila-based cocktail comes with a colorful secret that's sure to amaze and delight.

The Trickster's Treat isn't just a cocktail—it's a mesmerizing experience. Featuring butterfly pea extract, this vibrant drink hides a magical transformation. When a shot of zesty lemon juice is added, the acidity works its wonders, shifting the cocktail's hue from a serene blue to a vivid purple. It's part science, part sorcery, and entirely enchanting.

Perfect for surprising guests or adding whimsy to your celebrations, the Trickster's Treat combines delicious flavor with a touch of theatrical flair. Raise your glass to the unexpected, the fun, and a bit of cocktail magic that's sure to leave everyone smiling.

1. *Rim a coupe glass with salt (learn how to rim a glass on page 19) and some water.*

2. *In a cocktail shaker, combine the tequila, triple sec, butterfly pea flower extract, and a pinch of edible glitter along with a handful of ice cubes.*

3. *Shake until cool, then strain into the rimmed and chilled coupe glass.*

4. *Next, squeeze the fresh lemon juice into a shot glass. When you want to show off the cocktail's color-changing properties, pour it in.*

PREPARATION TIME:
5 minutes

GLASSWARE:
Coupe glass and shot glass

CELEBRATION:
April Fools' Day

SERVES: 1

2 ounces (60 ml) tequila

1 ounce (30 ml) triple sec

2 to 3 tablespoons (10 to 15 drops) butterfly pea flower extract

Pinch of edible glitter

Ice cubes

1 ounce (30 ml) fresh lemon juice

GARNISH:
Salt, to rim the glass

BARTENDER TIP: The butterfly pea flower extract works as a natural pH indicator and will react to the increase in acidity from the lemon juice by changing the color of the drink!

BABY YO-DAIQUIRI

PREPARATION TIME:
5 minutes

GLASSWARE:
Coupe glass

CELEBRATION:
Star Wars Day

SERVES: 1

2 ounces (60 ml)
light rum

2 ounces (60 ml)
melon liqueur

2 ounces (60 ml)
fresh lime juice

Ice cubes

GARNISH:
Two lime wedges (ears),
burlap napkin, two
blueberries, and a cocktail
stick (for eyes)

NO MAY THE FOURTH CELEBRATION is complete without a cocktail as adorable as it is delicious! The Baby Yo-Daiquiri is the ultimate tribute to Star Wars Day, uniting fans across the galaxy with its sweet, refreshing charm and a playful nod to everyone's favorite pint-sized Jedi-in-training.

With its vibrant colors and stellar flavor, this fruit daiquiri is a true showstopper. Don't be fooled by its small size—the force is strong with this one! A stellar blend of melon liqueur and light rum creates a drink that's as delightful to sip as it is to behold.

Whether you're rewatching the saga, raising a toast to your favorite Jedi, or simply channeling your inner Mandalorian, the Baby Yo-Daiquiri will take your May the Fourth festivities to a whole new galaxy. Cheers, and may the force be with you!

1. *First, tie the napkin around the glass to form the robe of the Baby Yo-Daiquiri. Next add the two blueberries on a cocktail stick for eyes and two lime slices for ears.*

2. *For the cocktail, combine the rum, melon liqueur, and lime juice in a cocktail shaker along with a handful of ice cubes. Shake until cool and strain into the decorated chilled coupe glass.*

CINCO DE MAYO MARGARITA

CINCO DE MAYO, CELEBRATED EVERY MAY 5, honors Mexico's historic victory over the Second French Empire at the Battle of Puebla in 1862. Today, it's a vibrant celebration of Mexican culture, marked by delicious cuisine, colorful parades, lively dances, and, of course, margaritas—the quintessential fiesta drink!

No Cinco de Mayo celebration is complete without this homemade margarita recipe, crafted to perfection for any occasion. This is truly the ultimate margarita—easy to make and endlessly customizable, catering to any taste with different spice levels. Whether you're mixing up a single glass or preparing a pitcher for friends, this fresh, flavorful margarita will leave premade mixes in the dust.

Celebrate Cinco de Mayo in style and raise a glass to the rich heritage of Mexico with this crowd-pleasing cocktail. One sip, and you'll be hooked. Cheers to a fiesta full of flavor and fun!

1. *With a mortar and pestle, grind the salt, chili powder and smoked paprika. Rim the margarita glasses with spicy salt and water (learn how to rim a glass on page 19).*

2. *In a cocktail shaker combine the tequila, fresh grapefruit juice, triple sec, lime juice, simple syrup (see recipe on page 40), and two handfuls of ice cubes. Add in a few jalapeño slices if you like it extra spicy. Shake vigorously until the mixture is cool.*

3. *Carefully stain the margarita mixture into a pitcher or straight into the prepared rimmed glasses and garnish with a lime wheel.*

PREPARATION TIME:
10 minutes

GLASSWARE:
Pitcher and margarita glass

CELEBRATION:
Cinco de Mayo

SERVES: 4

8 ounces (235 ml) blanco tequila

8 ounces (235 ml) fresh grapefruit juice

4 ounces (120 ml) triple sec

4 ounces (120 ml) lime juice

2 ounces (60 ml) simple syrup (see recipe on page 40)

4 to 8 slices of fresh jalapeño (optional, for extra spice)

Ice cubes

GARNISH:
8 tablespoons (144 g) salt, 4 teaspoons (10 g) chili powder, 4 teaspoons (10 g) smoked paprika, and lime wheels

MOTHER'S DAY BLOOM

PREPARATION TIME:
5 minutes

GLASSWARE:
Coupe glass

CELEBRATION:
Mother's Day

SERVES: 1

1½ ounces (45 ml)
lavender-infused gin

½ ounce (15 ml)
elderflower liqueur

1 ounce (30 ml)
fresh lemon juice

1 ounce (30 ml)
lavender and rose syrup
(see recipe on page 42)

½ ounce (15 ml) egg white

Ice cubes

GARNISH:
Edible rose petals

THIS MOTHER'S DAY, TREAT the most extraordinary woman in your life to a cocktail as graceful and unique as she is: the Mother's Day Bloom. With its soft pink hue and enchanting floral flavors, this elegant creation is destined to be the star of your celebratory brunch.

A harmonious blend of botanical gin, fragrant elderflower, and a touch of lavender and rose syrup, this cocktail blooms like a delicate bouquet with every sip. Garnished with elegant rose petals, it's the perfect complement to the flowers you've thoughtfully chosen for the special day.

More than just a drink, the Mother's Day Bloom is a celebration of a mother's unwavering love and support—a beautiful way to say "thank you" for everything she does. Sip, savor, and secure your spot as her favorite this year.

1. *Combine the lavender-infused gin, elderflower liqueur, fresh lemon juice, and lavender and rose syrup (see recipe on page 42) into a cocktail shaker along with a handful of ice cubes. Shake until cold and the egg white is frothy.*

2. *Carefully strain the cocktail into a chilled coupe glass.*

3. *Garnish with a scattering of edible rose petals.*

3

Summer
BREEZES &
SUNSET PARTIES

THIS CHAPTER IS YOUR INVITATION to embrace the warmth, vibrancy, and carefree spirit of summer through a collection of refreshing cocktails designed for every occasion. Summer is a season of connection and celebration, where hosting becomes an art of creating unforgettable moments. Whether you're throwing a Pride-themed extravaganza, channeling beachside bliss, hosting a backyard barbecue, or enjoying a relaxed picnic under the sun, a signature cocktail is the perfect way to set the tone and elevate your gathering.

A great summer cocktail ties your party's theme together, showcasing bold flavors and vibrant presentations that capture the joy of the season. From timeless classics like citrusy margaritas, refreshing mojitos, and the ever-charming Aperol Spritz, to innovative creations featuring fresh, seasonal ingredients, there's no shortage of inspiration. Juicy watermelons, zesty lemons, fragrant mint, and sweet tropical fruits like pineapple and mango take center stage, offering a burst of summer's finest flavors with every sip.

Whether shaken, stirred, or blended to frosty perfection, these cocktails are crafted to cool, refresh, and delight. From poolside spritzes to festival toasts and everything in between, these drinks are your ticket to making every summer celebration as vibrant and unforgettable as the season itself.

DAD'S OLD-FASHIONED

THIS FATHER'S DAY, skip the socks and ties and give your dad a gift he'll truly savor—a perfectly crafted old-fashioned. This timeless cocktail is a bold and sophisticated mix of smooth bourbon with a hint of sweetness from sugar and a touch of aromatic bitters, all garnished with a classic twist of orange peel.

Much like Dad himself, the old-fashioned is strong and dependable, with just the right amount of classic charm. It's the perfect way to toast to his wisdom, wit, and, of course, those unforgettable dad jokes.

1. *Place the sugar cube in the bottom of a chilled rocks glass and add 2 to 3 dashes of bitters on top of the sugar.*

2. *Add a small splash of water (about a teaspoon) to help dissolve the sugar.*

3. *Use a muddler or spoon to gently muddle the ingredients together until the sugar dissolves and the mixture is well combined.*

4. *Add the bourbon and large ice cubes and stir gently with a bar spoon until the mixture is chilled.*

5. *Garnish with a strip of orange peel, expressing the citrus oils by gently twisting it over the glass, then drop it into the drink.*

PREPARATION TIME:
5 minutes

GLASSWARE:
Rocks glass

CELEBRATION:
Father's Day

SERVES: 1

1 sugar cube

2 to 3 dashes bitters

1 teaspoon water

Large ice cubes

2 ounces (60 ml) bourbon

GARNISH:
Orange peel

SUNSHINE SANGRIA

PREPARATION TIME:
10 minutes

GLASSWARE:
Pitcher and mason jars

CELEBRATION:
Summer solstice

SERVES: 6 to 8

2 lemons (cut into
thin slices)

2 limes (cut into
thin slices)

8 fresh strawberries,
hulled and sliced

1 orange (cut into
thin slices)

Several roughly
torn mint leaves

6 ounces (175 ml)
agave nectar syrup

5 ounces (150 ml)
silver tequila

2 ounces (60 ml)
fresh lime juice

1 bottle red wine

Ice cubes

Soda water

GARNISH:
Torn mint leaves

CELEBRATE THE LONGEST DAY OF THE YEAR
and bask in the golden glow of summer with the
Sunshine Sangria by your side. This vibrant cocktail is
a harmonious blend of zesty citrus, luscious summer
fruits, and full-bodied rich red wine, creating a drink as
radiant and refreshing as the midsummer sun.

Whether you're relaxing poolside, hosting a garden
party, or savoring a tranquil evening on the patio, this
sangria perfectly captures the spirit of the warmth, light,
and joy of the summer solstice.

1. *In a large pitcher combine 2 to 3 handfuls of ice with
   the sliced fruit, mint leaves, agave nectar syrup,
   tequila, lime juice, and red wine.*

2. *Give the mixture a vigorous stir and top with soda
   water. Allow the cocktail to chill in the fridge for at
   least an hour before serving.*

3. *To serve, pour the cocktail into a pitcher filled with
   ice cubes. Divide it into mason jars and garnish each
   with a few torn mint leaves.*

TROPICAL GETAWAY

ESCAPE TO A WORLD OF SUN-KISSED SHORES and ocean breezes with the Tropical Getaway—a tiki cocktail that embodies the spirit of summer vacations. Whether you're strolling along a sandy beach, collecting seashells, or simply soaking up the sun from your backyard, this vibrant drink is your perfect companion for paradise.

The Tropical Getaway blends light and golden rum with a medley of tropical fruit juices, delivering a burst of island flavor. The nutty sweetness of orgeat syrup adds a hint of indulgence, while a drizzle of grenadine creates a stunning sunset effect in every glass—a reminder of the fiery hues over an endless ocean.

The fun of a tiki cocktail lies in the garnishes—pile on the pineapple, cherries, and citrus slices—and a festive miniature cocktail umbrella.

1. *In a cocktail shaker combine the rums, juices, and orgeat syrup along with a handful of ice cubes. Shake vigorously until the mixture is cool.*

2. *Fill a tiki glass halfway with crushed ice, then strain the mixture into the glass.*

3. *Using the back of a spoon, gently pour grenadine along the inside edge of the glass to create a layer at the bottom.*

4. *Garnish with a fresh pineapple slice, pineapple leaves, and a tropical paper umbrella for an extra touch of summer flair.*

PREPARATION TIME:
5 minutes

GLASSWARE:
Tiki glass

CELEBRATION:
Summer vacation

SERVES: 1

1 ounce (30 ml) golden rum

1 ounce (30 ml) white rum

2 ounces (60 ml) pineapple juice

2 ounces (60 ml) fresh orange juice

½ ounce (15 ml) fresh lime juice

½ ounce (15 ml) orgeat syrup

A drizzle of grenadine syrup

Ice cubes

Crushed ice

GARNISH:
Pineapple leaves, pineapple slice, and a cocktail umbrella

RAINBOW PARADISE

PREPARATION TIME:
10 minutes

GLASSWARE:
Hurricane glass

CELEBRATION:
Pride

SERVES: 1

1 ounce (30 ml) grenadine syrup

½ ounce (15 ml) blue curaçao

1 ounce (30 ml) water

4 ounces (120 ml) pineapple juice

2 ounces (60 ml) coconut rum

Crushed ice

Ice cubes

GARNISH:
Orange wheel on the rim of the glass and a rainbow belt candy onto a cocktail stick to represent the Pride flag

IF YOU'RE COMING OUT TO CELEBRATE PRIDE this June, then there's only one cocktail that will be serving realness and have all your friends ogling in awe! Introducing the fabulous Rainbow Paradise—a dazzling, multi-layered cocktail that's a true tribute to the vibrancy and joy of Pride celebrations! Inspired by the iconic rainbow flag, this drink captures the essence of love, unity, and all the fun of Pride.

The colorful layers of grenadine, pineapple juice, and blue curaçao come together to create a striking visual masterpiece that is not only bold and beautiful, but delicious too. Topped with a rainbow candy belt symbolizing the iconic Pride flag, the Rainbow Paradise is perfect for toasting to love, friendship, or simply a great time. This colorful, tropical treat celebrates the beauty of the rainbow in every sip!

1. *Pour the grenadine syrup into the bottom of a glass and set aside.*

2. *Fill the glass with crushed ice to create a solid base for layering.*

3. *In a separate glass, mix the blue curaçao with water and stir until fully combined.*

4. *Slowly pour the blue curaçao mixture over the back of a spoon or gently down the side of the glass to form the middle layer.*

5. *Combine the pineapple juice and coconut rum into a cocktail shaker with a handful of ice cubes and shake vigorously until the mixture is cool.*

6. *Strain the mixture into the glass, pouring slowly over the back of a spoon or gently down the side to preserve the two layers.*

FESTIVAL FIZZ

THE FESTIVAL FIZZ IS YOUR ULTIMATE FESTIVAL companion, capturing the spirit of adventure and good vibes wherever the music takes you. This is a cocktail built for the free-spirited, designed to keep things simple when you're miles away from the comforts of home—no kitchen, no ice, no shaker needed.

Inspired by the bold kick of a Long Island iced tea, the Festival Fizz is a tangy, potent mix that's ready to party. Just premix the base, toss it in your bag, and when the moment's right, crack open a cold can of cola to bring the cocktail to life.

Whether you're deep in the woods or soaking up the electric buzz of a festival crowd, the Festival Fizz brings big flavor and big fun, all without breaking a sweat. Raise a cup and let the good times flow! (Just be sure to check rules about alcohol at the site!)

1. *In a clean bottle or container, combine all the liquid ingredients (rum, gin, vodka, tequila, triple sec, and simple syrup [see recipe on page 40]).*

2. *Seal the container tightly and shake to combine. This is your premixed Long Island iced tea base. Chill it in your fridge or pack it into a cooler with your festival or camping supplies.*

3. *When you're ready to serve at the festival or campsite, grab your cold can of cola and your premixed base. Add the fresh lemon and lime juice to the base, then gently shake the bottle—using it as a makeshift cocktail shaker—to bring the drink together.*

4. *Pour the mixture into a cup (about three-quarters of the cup) and add a few ice cubes if you have them handy.*

5. *Top up with the cold cola and stir gently to combine.*

PREPARATION TIME:
10 minutes

GLASSWARE:
Cups

CELEBRATION:
Festival or camping

SERVES: 4

Cocktail mixture (to be prepared at home):

2 ounces (60 ml) light rum

2 ounces (60 ml) gin

2 ounces (60 ml) vodka

2 ounces (60 ml) light tequila

2 ounces (60 ml) triple sec

2 ounces (60 ml) simple syrup (see recipe on page 40)

At the site:

2 ounces (60 ml) fresh lemon juice

2 ounces (60 ml) fresh lime juice

Top up with cold can of cola

Ice cubes (optional)

GARNISH:
Sprig of mint and lemon wheel

BARTENDER TIP:
Gently clap the mint leaves between your hands before adding them to your drink. This technique helps to release the essential oils without bruising the leaves too much, which can lead to a bitter taste.

SUMMER JAMMER

PREPARATION TIME:
5 minutes

GLASSWARE:
Jam or mason jar,
or collins glass

CELEBRATION:
Summer picnic

SERVES: 1

2 ounces (60 ml) gin

2 tablespoons (40 g)
seedless strawberry jam

½ ounce (15 ml)
fresh lemon juice

3 to 4 mint leaves

Ice cubes

Club soda

GARNISH:
Strawberries, halved;
mint sprig

CAPTURE THE ESSENCE OF SUMMER with the Summer Jammer, a refreshing gin-based cocktail inspired by the nostalgic sweetness of strawberry jam. This delightful drink combines ripe, juicy strawberries, smooth gin, and a sparkling splash of club soda, creating a perfect balance of fruity freshness and fizzy fun.

Served in a charming jam jar, the Summer Jammer brings a rustic, playful vibe to your outdoor gatherings while offering unmatched convenience. With its screw-on lid, it's picnic-ready and easy to transport, whether you're lounging by the lake or relaxing in your backyard.

As you stretch out on your picnic blanket or gather with friends, the Summer Jammer delivers the perfect blend of refreshment and charm. Sip, savor, and soak in the sunshine with this jammy little cocktail—a sweet companion for all your summer adventures.

IF USING A JAM OR MASON JAR:

1. *Combine the gin, strawberry jam, lemon juice, and torn mint leaves in the jar with a handful of ice cubes.*

2. *Secure the lid of the jar tightly and shake vigorously until chilled.*

3. *Top with club soda and screw the lid back on for easy transport to your picnic.*

IF USING A COLLINS GLASS:

1. *In a cocktail shaker, combine the gin, strawberry jam, and lemon juice with a handful of ice cubes. Shake vigorously until chilled.*

2. *Fill a glass halfway with ice cubes and 3 to 4 torn mint leaves. Pour the chilled cocktail mixture into the glass, top with club soda, and stir well with a bar spoon.*

SUNSET SPRITZ

TRANSPORT YOURSELF TO THE GOLDEN warmth of an Italian piazza with the Sunset Spritz. Inspired by the iconic Aperol Spritz, this cocktail combines the perfect balance of crisp prosecco, bittersweet Aperol, and a splash of sparkling soda to create a refreshing burst of citrusy goodness. With every sip, feel the sun setting over the cobblestone streets as the vibrant orange hue of the drink mirrors the glowing skies of an endless afternoon. Whether you're lounging on a terrace or enjoying a laid-back moment, let the Sunset Spritz be your passport to a carefree, sun-drenched escape.

1. *Fill a large wine glass with ice cubes.*

2. *Pour in the Aperol, prosecco, and soda water. Using a bar spoon, gently stir the ingredients to combine.*

3. *Add a vibrant wheel of blood orange to the glass for a pop of color and citrus aroma.*

PREPARATION TIME:
5 minutes

GLASSWARE:
Large wine glass

CELEBRATION:
Summer BBQ

SERVES: 1

3 ounces (90 ml) Aperol or other Italian orange aperitif

2 ounces (60 ml) prosecco (or any sparkling wine)

1 ounce (30 ml) soda water

Ice cubes

GARNISH:
Blood orange wheel

LA TOMATINA

PREPARATION TIME:
10 minutes

GLASSWARE:
Pitcher and mason jars

CELEBRATION:
La Tomatina festival

SERVES: 4

4 ounces (120 ml) vodka

16 ounces (475 ml)
tomato juice

1 ounce (30 ml)
fresh lemon juice

1 ounce (30 ml)
of Worcestershire sauce

2 to 3 dashes
of hot sauce

Pinch of celery salt

Pinch of smoked paprika

Pinch of black pepper

Crushed ice

GARNISH:
Celery stick and
a slice of lemon

CHANNEL THE SPIRITED CHAOS of Spain's iconic La Tomatina festival with the La Tomatina cocktail—a savory, vibrant twist on the classic Bloody Mary. Every August, the streets of Buñol, Spain, erupt into a joyous frenzy as thousands of revelers partake in the world's largest tomato-throwing celebration. This lively event inspired a cocktail that's as bold and unforgettable as the festival itself.

The La Tomatina cocktail captures the essence of this exuberant tradition with its rich and savory profile. Fresh tomato juice provides natural sweetness, complemented by the zesty brightness of lemon and a fiery kick from hot sauce and Worcestershire sauce. The result is a perfectly balanced drink that's equal parts indulgent and invigorating.

Whether you're hosting a themed party, adding flair to your brunch, or simply craving something adventurous, the La Tomatina cocktail brings a playful burst of flavor to any occasion. *Cin cin!*

1. *Place crushed ice in a pitcher and pour in the vodka, tomato juice, and lemon juice over the ice.*

2. *Add the Worcestershire source, hot sauce, celery salt, smoked paprika, and black pepper. Stir until the outside of the pitcher feels cold.*

3. *Serve in a mason jar and garnish with a celery stick and a slice of lemon.*

MAPLE LEAF MARTINI

WITH CANADA PROUDLY PRODUCING more than 70 percent of the world's maple syrup, what better way to celebrate Canada Day (July 1) than with the Maple Leaf Martini—a cocktail as quintessentially Canadian as the red maple leaf itself. This delightful creation blends the smoothness of premium vodka, the citrusy brightness of triple sec, and the rich, golden sweetness of pure maple syrup, delivering a drink that's as warm and inviting as the True North.

Whether you're dreaming of your next adventure in Canada, cheering on a hockey game, or humming along to "O Canada," the Maple Leaf Martini is the perfect way to raise a glass to all the things that make Canada extraordinary. Sip it under the glow of fireworks, savor its sweet charm, and celebrate the True North strong, proud, and deliciously sweet. Cheers, eh!

1. *Rim a martini glass (learn how to rim a glass on page 19) with the brown sugar and maple syrup.*

2. *Combine the vodka, maple syrup, triple sec, and lemon juice into a cocktail shaker with a handful of ice cubes and shake vigorously until the mixture is cool.*

3. *Carefully strain the cocktail into your sugar-rimmed martini glass and garnish with a lemon twist.*

PREPARATION TIME:
5 minutes

GLASSWARE:
Martini glass

CELEBRATION:
Canada Day

SERVES: 1

1 tablespoon (20 g) maple syrup for decorating the glass

2 ounces (60 ml) vodka

1 ounce (28 g) maple syrup

½ ounce (15 ml) triple sec

1 ounce (30 ml) fresh lemon juice

Ice cubes

GARNISH:
Brown sugar (for rimming) and a lemon twist

PATRIOTIC PUNCH

PREPARATION TIME:
10 minutes

GLASSWARE:
Punch bowl and tumblers

CELEBRATION:
Independence Day

SERVES: 8 to 12

8 ounces (235 ml)
cherry juice

12 ounces (355 ml) vodka

3 ounces (90 ml)
raspberry liqueur

1 ounce (30 ml)
fresh lime juice

1 ounce (30 ml)
fresh lemon juice

12 ounces (355 ml),
1 can, cherry
sparkling water

12 ounces (355 ml),
1 can, ginger beer

Ice cubes

GARNISH:
Blueberries, maraschino
cherries, and apple
cut into star shapes

CELEBRATE INDEPENDENCE DAY in star-spangled style with the Patriotic Punch! As American as apple pie, this vibrant cocktail features red cranberry juice, sweet blueberries, and crisp apple stars to garnish—perfectly capturing the red, white, and blue spirit of July Fourth.

This festive punch is perfect for Independence Day gatherings, where friends and family can serve themselves with ease, savoring good food, lively conversations, and the dazzling fireworks lighting up the night sky. It's a celebration in a glass, adding a refreshing splash of patriotism to your Fourth of July festivities!

1. *To prepare the garnish, cut the apple into thin slices and use a small star-shaped cutter to create apple stars. Wash the blueberries and set them aside, along with the maraschino cherries.*

2. *In a large punch bowl, combine the cherry juice, vodka, raspberry liqueur, lime juice, and lemon juice.*

3. *Slowly pour in the cherry sparkling water and ginger beer, stirring gently to preserve the fizz.*

4. *Add enough ice cubes to chill the punch.*

5. *Pour the punch into tumblers and garnish each with a few blueberries, a maraschino cherry, and a couple of apple star slices for a patriotic red, white, and blue touch.*

4

Autumn
ALCHEMY & HARVEST
FESTIVITIES

AUTUMN USHERS IN A SEASON OF WARMTH, togetherness, and vibrant celebrations as the crisp air and fiery foliage set the perfect backdrop for gatherings of all kinds. From hauntingly fun Halloween parties decked out in spooky decor, to heartfelt Thanksgiving dinners filled with gratitude, fall is a time to revel in the beauty of the season and connect with loved ones.

A well-crafted cocktail can elevate these cherished moments, aligning perfectly with the flavors and themes of the season. Autumnal classics like the Old-Fashioned, spiced cider, and hot toddy bring to mind cozy evenings by the fire, with their warming spices—cinnamon, nutmeg, and clove—capturing the heart of fall. Flavors like maple, apple, pear, and pumpkin spice evoke nostalgia and comfort, while robust spirits like whiskey, dark rum, and brandy form the perfect base for these rich, seasonal sips.

This chapter invites you to savor the essence of fall with cocktails that celebrate the season's bounty, flavors, and atmosphere. Whether you're hosting a lively Oktoberfest celebration or a quiet evening by the fire, these drinks will help you embrace the magic of autumn and make every gathering unforgettable.

PUMPKINTINI

AS THE LEAVES TURN GOLDEN and the air grows crisp, there's nothing quite like sipping on a cocktail that captures the essence of autumn and the changing of seasons. The Pumpkintini, served in an elegant martini glass, is a delightful twist on your favorite holiday pumpkin pie, making it the perfect addition to any fall gathering.

The Pumpkintini is not just a drink; it's a celebration of the season. With real pumpkin puree, a hint of maple syrup, and a sprinkle of pumpkin spice, this martini embodies all the comforting flavors of pumpkin pie, but in a chic, chilled glass. It's rich and decadent, with nuances of whiskey and rum that add warmth and complexity. So, put away the pie dish—this is Thanksgiving in a glass, minus the hours spent in the kitchen!

1. *Start by rimming your martini glass with the cinnamon-sugar mixture and a little water (learn how to rim a glass on page 19).*

2. *Combine the vodka, pumpkin puree, maple syrup, heavy cream, whiskey, and pumpkin spice into a cocktail shaker along with a handful of ice cubes and shake vigorously until the mixture is cool.*

3. *Strain the mixture carefully into the rimmed martini glass.*

4. *Garnish with a sprinkle of cinnamon and a cinnamon stick on top.*

PREPARATION TIME:
5 minutes

GLASSWARE:
Martini glass

CELEBRATION:
Fall/Thanksgiving

SERVES: 1

2 ounces (60 ml) vodka

1 ounce (30 ml) pumpkin puree (or pumpkin pie filling)

1 ounce (28 g) maple syrup

1 ounce (30 ml) heavy cream

½ ounce (15 ml) whiskey

½ teaspoon pumpkin spice syrup

Ice cubes

GARNISH:
1 tablespoon (13 g) sugar and ½ teaspoon ground cinnamon for rimming the glass, and a sprinkle of cinnamon with a cinnamon stick

BAVARIAN SHANDY

PREPARATION TIME:
5 minutes

GLASSWARE:
Stein or tankard

CELEBRATION:
Oktoberfest

SERVES: 1

1 bottle wheat beer

4 ounces (120 ml) ginger beer

2 to 3 lemon slices

A few fresh mint leaves

Ice cubes

GARNISH:
Mint sprig

THE MONTH OF OCTOBER can only mean one thing on the drinking calendar—Oktoberfest! What began in 1810 as a royal wedding celebration in Munich has evolved into a worldwide festival of Bavarian culture, complete with lively oompah bands, traditional lederhosen, and mouthwatering bratwurst. While beer remains the heart of the celebration, beer-infused cocktails are bringing a fresh and creative twist to the festivities.

This year, elevate your Oktoberfest experience with a refreshing Bavarian Shandy. This modern take combines the crisp smoothness of wheat beer with the zesty spice of ginger beer, finished with fragrant mint leaves for an aromatic flourish. It's a perfectly balanced cocktail that beer enthusiasts and cocktail lovers can equally enjoy.

Whether you're raising your glass at a bustling beer garden or hosting your own Oktoberfest-inspired party, this delightful shandy will transport you straight to Bavaria. So, don your dirndl or lederhosen, gather your friends, and toast to good times and great flavors. *Prost!*

1. Fill a beer stein or large glass halfway with ice.

2. Pour the wheat beer over the ice, filling the glass about three-quarters full. Top it up with ginger beer.

3. Add the lemon slices and fresh mint leaves and gently stir to combine the ingredients.

4. Garnish with an extra sprig of mint for a fresh finish.

SPICY SUGAR SKULL PALOMA

CELEBRATE THE RICH TRADITIONS and vibrant energy of Día de los Muertos (Day of the Dead) with the Spicy Sugar Skull Paloma—a bold, festive twist on the classic Mexican cocktail. This spirited drink embodies the heart of the holiday, blending the smoothness of tequila with the tangy brightness of fresh grapefruit juice and a touch of honey syrup for sweetness. A dash of chili spice adds just the right amount of heat, creating a flavor profile as lively as the celebrations themselves.

With its chili-salt rim, vibrant grapefruit wedge, and colorful flowers inspired by the flower crowns of Día de los Muertos, the Spicy Sugar Skull Paloma is a stunning creation.

So, raise your glass to honor the cherished memories of loved ones, sharing in the joy and reflection that define this meaningful holiday. This cocktail isn't just a drink— it's a celebration of life, love, and the enduring spirit of those who came before us. ¡Salud!

1. *Rim a highball glass (learn how to rim a glass on page 19) using a seasoning, such as Tajín, and water.*

2. *In a cocktail shaker, add the fresh jalapeño slice and gently muddle to release the spicy oils.*

3. *Next add the tequila, fresh lime juice, honey syrup (see recipe on page 41), and a pink grapefruit juice into the cocktail shaker along with a handful of ice cubes and shake vigorously until the mixture is cool.*

4. *Carefully strain the mixture into the prepared rimmed glass.*

5. *Add a few ice cubes and top up with soda water and garnish with a grapefruit wedge.*

PREPARATION TIME:
5 minutes

GLASSWARE:
Highball glass

CELEBRATION:
Día de los Muertos

SERVES: 1

1 to 2 slices fresh jalapeño

2 ounces (60 ml) blanco or reposado tequila

1 ounce (30 ml) fresh lime juice

½ ounce (15 ml) honey syrup (see recipe on page 41)

2 ounces (60 ml) pink grapefruit juice

Soda water

Ice cubes

GARNISH:
Seasoning, such as Tajín; bright edible flowers; and a pink grapefruit wedge

BARTENDER TIP:

Marigolds, traditionally associated with Día de los Muertos celebrations, are a versatile addition to the culinary world. With their tangy, slightly peppery flavor, edible marigold petals make an exceptional garnish for this cocktail, adding both visual flair and a unique taste.

SMOKY S'MORE MARTINI

PREPARATION TIME:
10 minutes

GLASSWARE:
Martini glass

CELEBRATION:
Camping trip

SERVES: 1

1 tablespoon (20 g)
maple syrup for
decorating the glass

2 ounces (60 ml)
chocolate liqueur

1 ounce (30 ml) vodka

½ ounce (15 ml)
marshmallow syrup or
simple syrup (see recipe
on page 40 or 43)

1 ounce (30 ml)
heavy cream

Ice cubes

GARNISH:
Chocolate sauce, crushed
graham crackers, maple
syrup, and a marshmallow

READY TO TAKE YOUR CAMPING TRIP from
rugged to refined? Step into the world of glamping
with the Smoky S'more Martini—a cocktail that
transforms the beloved campfire treat into a luxurious,
grown-up indulgence.

This decadent drink combines the velvety richness
of chocolate liqueur, the smoky warmth of toasted
marshmallow, and the crunch of a graham cracker rim,
capturing the essence of s'mores in every sip. Perfect for
savoring under the stars or beside a crackling fire, the
Smoky S'more Martini adds a touch of elegance to your
outdoor adventures while keeping the nostalgic charm of
campfire memories alive.

Whether you're unwinding after a day of exploring or
simply soaking in the magic of the night sky, this cocktail
is your ticket to ultimate campfire bliss.

1. *Rim a martini glass (learn how to rim a glass on
   page 19) with crushed graham crackers and maple
   syrup. Drizzle chocolate sauce in a swirling pattern
   along the inside of the glass before setting aside to chill.*

2. *Combine the chocolate liqueur, vodka, marshmallow
   or simple syrup (see recipe on page 40 or 43), and heavy
   cream into a cocktail shaker with a handful of ice cubes
   and shake vigorously until the mixture is cool.*

3. *Carefully strain the cocktail into your graham
   cracker-rimmed martini glass and garnish with a
   toasted marshmallow on a cocktail stick.*

ZOMBIE-BRAIN SHOTS

THIS HALLOWEEN, THRILL YOUR GUESTS with the Zombie-Brain Shot—a spine-chilling concoction that's as delicious as it is delightfully creepy. Combining Irish cream liqueur, peach schnapps, and a splash of grenadine, this shot transforms into a ghastly "brain" effect, perfect for a mad scientist's laboratory or a haunted house party.

Its eerie, curdled appearance may give you goosebumps, but the wickedly sweet flavor will keep your guests coming back for more. Whether you're hosting a monster mash or a ghostly gathering, the Zombie-Brain Shot is the ultimate party potion to set the stage for a night of spooktacular fun. Serve up these creepy creations and watch them become the scream of the evening!

1. *Pour the chilled schnapps into a shot glass.*

2. *Gently pour the Irish cream liqueur over the back of a spoon, allowing it to float on top of the peach schnapps (learn how to layer on page 19).*

3. *Carefully drop the grenadine into the shot. It will sink to the bottom but create a "brain-like" appearance as it interacts with the cream.*

4. *Repeat the steps above until you have the desired number of shots prepared.*

PREPARATION TIME:
10 minutes

GLASSWARE:
Shot glass

CELEBRATION:
Halloween

SERVES: 1

1 ounce (30 ml) peach schnapps

½ ounce (15 ml) Irish cream liqueur

½ ounce (15 ml) grenadine syrup

WITCHES' BREW PUNCH

PREPARATION TIME
15 minutes

GLASSWARE
Cauldron and tumblers

CELEBRATION:
Halloween

SERVES: 8

32 ounces (950 ml)
fresh orange juice

16 ounces (475 ml)
fresh pineapple juice

8 ounces (235 ml)
fresh lime juice

8 ounces (235 ml) vodka

8 ounces (235 ml)
white rum

16 ounces (475 ml)
lemon-lime soda

Black food coloring

Block ice

GARNISH:
1 can of lychees,
1 jar of maraschino
cherries, 1 small
bag of raisins

CONJURE UP SOME HALLOWEEN MAGIC with the Witches' Brew Punch, a spooky yet scrumptious centerpiece for your haunted gathering. Served in a cauldron for that authentic witchy vibe, this eerie punch combines the inky darkness of vodka with black food coloring and the fizz of ginger ale with the tang of fruit juices, delivering a refreshing potion that's as flavorful as it is frightful. The addition of floating lychee "eyeballs" elevates the spooky spectacle, adding creepy charm and a surprisingly sweet treat for the brave souls who dare to indulge.

Whether you're hosting a graveyard bash or dancing the skeleton shuffle, the Witches' Brew is your ticket to a frightfully fabulous celebration.

1. *In a cauldron or large punch bowl, combine the orange juice, pineapple juice, and lime juice. Stir gently to mix the juices.*

2. *Pour in the vodka, white rum, and stir again to combine, adding several drops of black food coloring to give an eerie vibe to the concoction.*

3. *Slowly pour in the lemon-lime soda and gently stir.*

4. *Add the block ice and chill the punch until the party.*

5. *To garnish the tumblers, prepare edible eyeballs by draining the can of lychees and pat the fruit dry. With a cocktail stick, carefully poke a hole into each maraschino cherry. Insert a cherry into each lychee, making sure it fits snugly.*

6. *Insert a raisin into the center of the cherry to create the "pupil" of the eyeball. Place the completed eyeball onto a cocktail stick. Repeat for as many eyeballs as needed for your party.*

DIWALI DELIGHT

CELEBRATE THE FESTIVAL OF LIGHTS with the dazzling Diwali Delight, a cocktail that captures the essence of this vibrant celebration. Crafted with spiced rum and sweet mango, and infused with the aromatic warmth of cardamom, cloves, and ginger, this drink is a harmonious blend of tradition and indulgence.

Topped with golden accents and adorned with marigold petals—symbols of prosperity and positivity—the Diwali Delight sparkles like the festival itself. As gold glitter swirls within the glass, it mirrors the brilliance of fireworks lighting up the night sky, evoking the triumph of good over evil and the joyous spirit of Diwali in every luminous sip.

1. *Rim the glass using water and edible gold glitter (learn how to rim a glass on page 19).*

2. *Combine the spiced rum, mango juice, simple syrup (see recipe on page 40), spices, and edible gold glitter into a cocktail shaker along with a handful of ice cubes and shake vigorously until the mixture is cool.*

3. *Carefully strain the mixture into a prepared coupe glass. Garnish with edible flowers.*

BARTENDER TIP: Marigold flowers hold a special place in Diwali celebrations, symbolizing prosperity and positivity. Often used to create vibrant garlands and decorations, their bright hues are believed to invite good fortune—making them a meaningful and eye-catching garnish for this cocktail.

PREPARATION TIME:
5 minutes

GLASSWARE:
Coupe glass

CELEBRATION:
Diwali

SERVES: 1

1½ ounces (45 ml) spiced rum

2 ounces (60 ml) mango juice

½ ounce (15 ml) simple syrup (see recipe on page 40)

¼ teaspoon ground cardamom

Pinch of ground cloves

Pinch of ground ginger

Pinch of edible gold glitter

Ice cubes

GARNISH:

Edible gold glitter for rimming the glass and edible flowers

HARVEST PUNCH

PREPARATION TIME:
5 minutes

GLASSWARE:
Large punch bowl and tumblers

CELEBRATION:
Thanksgiving

SERVES: 8

32 ounces (950 ml) unsweetened cranberry juice

16 ounces (475 ml) bourbon

8 ounces (235 ml) amaretto liqueur

8 ounces (235 ml) orange juice

2 ounces (60 ml) lemon juice

4 cinnamon sticks

Ice cubes

GARNISH:
2 oranges, thinly sliced;
2 lemons, thinly sliced;
8 ounces (235 g) whole cranberries;
8 sprigs fresh rosemary

WHETHER YOU'RE HOSTING a traditional family feast or a casual potluck with friends, Harvest Punch is designed to bring people together. Its vibrant crimson hue mirrors the autumnal leaves, and its bold, spiced flavor is perfect for washing down a hearty Thanksgiving dinner—turkey, stuffing, and all.

Serve it in a punch bowl to let everyone ladle out a cup of holiday spirit, or by the glass for an elegant touch. However you enjoy it, Harvest Punch will be the toast of your celebration—raising a glass to good food, cherished company, and the spirit of gratitude!

1. *In a large punch bowl, combine the cranberry juice, bourbon, amaretto, orange juice, and lemon juice. Stir well to blend the ingredients.*

2. *Add 4 handfuls of ice cubes to cool the punch as well as the thinly sliced oranges and lemons, whole cranberries, and four cinnamon sticks. Stir gently to incorporate the fruit and spices into the punch.*

3. *Ladle the punch into glasses filled with ice. Garnish each glass with a sprig of fresh rosemary.*

5

Anytime

OCCASIONS: MILESTONES & MERRIMENT

LIFE IS FULL OF MILESTONES—big and small—that deserve to be celebrated. Whether it's the excitement of moving into a new home, the pride of landing that big promotion, the romance of getting engaged, or the joy of an anniversary, these moments are the highlights of our journey. And what better way to mark the occasion than with a signature cocktail that's as special as the moment itself?

Making cocktails for these milestones isn't just about pouring drinks; it's about creating something that tells a story. A housewarming cocktail can feel like the fresh start you're celebrating, a bachelorette drink can be as fun and sparkly as the bride-to-be, and a baby shower mocktail can be sweet and full of love. The right cocktail doesn't just set the tone—it makes the moment even more memorable, giving your guests something to sip, savor, and talk about long after the party ends.

But the true joy of hosting isn't found in perfection or presentation—it's in the connections we make. It's the shared laughter over a round of drinks, the music that fills the air, and the candid photos that capture smiles and clinking glasses. Parties are a chance to bring people together, celebrating life's moments with those who matter most. As you explore the cocktails in this chapter, let them inspire you to shake up something special for your next major milestone.

Here's to raising a glass, celebrating life's milestones, and creating memories as unforgettable as the cocktails themselves. Cheers to every moment worth toasting!

BIRTHDAY CAKE SHOTS

THIS FESTIVE CAKE-INSPIRED COCKTAIL is a must-have for any birthday celebration, combining the best of both booze and birthday cake in a single shot! Each shot glass is decorated with rainbow sprinkles and a swirl of whipped cream, making it as fun to look at as it is to drink. The combination of vanilla vodka, white chocolate liqueur, amaretto liqueur, and a splash of Irish cream liqueur come together to perfectly capture the delicious flavors of birthday cake!

Easy to prepare, crowd-pleasing, and bursting with celebratory cheer, this shot is the perfect way to kick off any birthday bash. Just don't forget to make a birthday wish before drinking! Sip sip hooray!

1. *Rim the shot glasses (learn how to rim a glass on page 19) with maple syrup and rainbow sprinkles.*

2. *Combine the vanilla vodka, Irish cream liqueur, white chocolate liqueur, amaretto liqueur, and light cream in a cocktail shaker along with a handful of ice cubes and shake vigorously until the mixture is cool.*

3. *Carefully strain the mixture into the prepared rimmed shot glasses. Garnish each shot with a small flourish of whipped cream.*

4. *Repeat the steps above until you have the desired number of shots prepared.*

PREPARATION TIME:
5 minutes

GLASSWARE:
Shot glasses

CELEBRATION:
Birthday celebrations

SERVES: 1

1 tablespoon (20 g) maple syrup for decorating the glass

1 ounce (30 ml) vanilla vodka

1 ounce (30 ml) Irish cream liqueur

1 ounce (30 ml) white chocolate liqueur

1 ounce (30 ml) amaretto liqueur

1 ounce (30 ml) light cream

Ice cubes

GARNISH:
Rainbow sprinkles and whipped cream

DIAMOND FIZZ

PREPARATION TIME:
5 minutes

GLASSWARE:
Champagne flute

CELEBRATION:
Engagement party

SERVES: 1

1 ounce (30 ml) gin

½ ounce (15 ml)
fresh lemon juice

½ ounce (15 ml)
simple syrup
(see recipe on page 40)

Champagne or
sparkling wine (chilled)

GARNISH:
Lemon twist and gold leaf

AN ENGAGEMENT PARTY calls for a cocktail as sparkling and joyful as the love it celebrates. With champagne as its star, this cocktail is made for toasting the happy couple and all the excitement of their journey ahead. A bright mix of gin and fresh citrus adds a crisp, refreshing twist, while the bubbles bring a touch of magic to every sip.

So, pop the bubbly, fill your flutes, and let the Diamond Fizz set the tone for a night of love, laughter, and unforgettable toasts. Here's to the happy couple, their journey together, and a cocktail worthy of the occasion.

1. *Combine the gin, fresh lemon juice, and simple syrup (see recipe on page 40) in a cocktail shaker along with a handful of ice cubes and shake vigorously until the mixture is cool.*

2. *Strain the mixture into a champagne flute and top with champagne or sparkling wine.*

3. *Garnish with a lemon twist and gold leaf for extra bling.*

BLUSHING BRIDE

THE BLUSHING BRIDE IS THE ULTIMATE cocktail to kick off a bachelorette party in style! This sparkling, pink concoction is as lively and vibrant as the night ahead, blending smooth vodka, sweet pomegranate liqueur, and a hint of rose water for a delightful floral twist. Topped with bubbly sparkling rosé, it's the perfect drink to toast to the bride-to-be.

This signature cocktail sets the tone for a night of fun, laughter, and happy-ever-after, so gather the Bride Tribe, don your sashes and pink attire, and get ready to dance the night away—because with the Blushing Bride in hand, the celebration has officially begun!

1. *Combine the vodka, pomegranate liqueur, simple syrup (see recipe on page 40), and a dash of rose water into a cocktail shaker along with a handful of ice cubes. Shake vigorously until the mixture is cool.*

2. *Carefully strain the cocktail into a champagne glass and top up with sparkling rosé wine.*

3. *Garnish with a few pomegranate seeds.*

PREPARATION TIME:
5 minutes

GLASSWARE:
Champagne glass

CELEBRATION:
Bachelorette party

SERVES: 1

1 ounce (30 ml) vodka

½ ounce (15 ml) pomegranate liqueur

½ ounce (15 ml) simple syrup (see recipe on page 40)

Dash of rose water

Sparkling rosé wine

Ice cubes

GARNISH:
Pomegranate seeds

MORTARBOARD MARTINI

PREPARATION TIME:
5 minutes

GLASSWARE:
Martini glass

CELEBRATION:
Graduation

SERVES: 1

2½ ounces (75 ml) bourbon

½ ounce (15 ml)
sweet vermouth

½ ounce (15 ml)
extra dry vermouth

2 dashes of orange bitters

Ice cubes

GARNISH:
Cherry and yellow
citrus peel

THE MORTARBOARD MARTINI is a sophisticated and celebratory twist on the classic Manhattan, created to honor graduates as they step into their next chapter. With a robust yet harmonious blend of whiskey, sweet vermouth, and bitters, this cocktail reflects the refinement and accomplishment earned through years of hard work and dedication. Each glass is garnished with a maraschino cherry and a bright yellow citrus peel tassel, a nod to the iconic mortarboard worn during the graduation ceremony.

The Mortarboard Martini is more than just a drink; it's a toast to late-night study marathons, the triumph over exams, and the growth that comes with every challenge faced along the way. Celebrate the journey, the milestones, and the bright future ahead with this elegant and spirited cocktail.

1. *Combine the bourbon, vermouth, and bitters in a mixing glass with a handful of ice cubes and stir until well chilled.*

2. *Strain into a chilled martini glass and garnish with a cherry on a cocktail stick, adorned with a strip of lemon citrus peel, finely cut into thin strips at one end to resemble the graduation cap tassel.*

HAPPILY EVER AFTER

HONORED GUESTS, PLEASE RAISE YOUR GLASSES to the Happily Ever After cocktail—a coconut martini as luminous as the lovebirds. This dazzling drink is a true celebration of love, blending the tropical allure of coconut rum, the smooth decadence of vanilla vodka, and the creamy richness of coconut cream. The glass, beautifully rimmed with delicate desiccated coconut, is a fitting nod to a bride's radiant white dress.

Perfect for rehearsal dinners, the Happily Ever After sets the tone for a weekend of romance and celebration. Cheers to love, laughter, and happily ever after!

1. *Rim the glass with maple syrup and desiccated coconut (learn how to rim a glass on page 19).*

2. *In a cocktail shaker, combine the vodka, rum, coconut cream, and pineapple juice with a handful of ice and shake vigorously until the mixture is cool.*

3. *Carefully strain the cocktail into the prepared chilled martini glass and garnish with white marshmallow.*

PREPARATION TIME:
5 minutes

GLASSWARE:
Martini glass

CELEBRATION:
Wedding day

SERVES: 1

1 tablespoon (20 g) of maple syrup for decorating the glass

1½ ounces (45 ml) vanilla vodka

1½ ounces (45 ml) coconut rum

2 ounces (60 ml) coconut cream

½ ounce (15 ml) pineapple juice

Ice cubes

GARNISH:
Desiccated coconut for rimming the glass and white marshmallows

OH, BABY

PREPARATION TIME:
5 minutes

GLASSWARE:
Champagne glass

CELEBRATION:
Baby shower

SERVES: 1

1 ounce (30 ml) vodka

1 ounce (30 ml)
elderflower syrup
(see recipe on page 41)

Dash of rose water

Sparkling white wine

Ice cubes

GARNISH:
Pink and blue cotton candy

THE OH, BABY COCKTAIL will soon be the most eagerly anticipated drink at any baby shower, bringing a perfect mix of celebration, excitement, and a playful twist! This festive drink is not just a toast to the soon-to-be parents, but also a playful way for guests to guess the baby's gender.

The Oh, Baby cocktail features a delightful blend of sparkling wine, floral elderflower syrup, and a dash of aromatic rose water. However, the real magic happens when guests add either a pink or blue cotton candy to their cocktail. This not only adds extra sweetness, it allows a colorful reveal of everyone's guess about the baby's gender. Guests can raise a glass of pink cocktail fizz if they are Team Girl or a glass of baby blue if they are Team Boy!

Don't forget to include the expectant mother-to-be too by whipping up a sparkling, nonalcoholic version so she can join in the fun! Let the guessing game begin as guests choose the color, adding a festive twist to a delicious cocktail. Get ready for a burst of flavor, color, and joy with this signature sip.

1. *Combine the vodka and elderflower syrup (see recipe on page 41), and a dash of rose water into a cocktail shaker along with a handful of ice cubes. Shake vigorously until the mixture is cool.*

2. *Carefully strain the cocktail into a chilled champagne glass and top with sparkling white wine.*

3. *Garnish with both blue and pink cotton candy, inviting guests to choose their color and stir it into the drink as a playful way to guess the baby's gender.*

TIMELESS LOVE

RAISE A GLASS TO ENDURING LOVE with the Timeless Love cocktail—a strawberry daiquiri created to celebrate the magic of anniversaries. This vibrant blend of fresh strawberries, bold rum, and a zesty hint of lime captures the perfect harmony of sweetness and strength, mirroring the bond that deepens with each passing year.

Whether shared over a candlelit dinner or during a quiet moment together, this cocktail sets the tone for an unforgettable celebration. From your first anniversary to your fiftieth, the Timeless Love is more than a drink—it's a toast to the laughter, joy, and cherished memories that define your journey together. Because with true love, every year is sweeter than the last.

1. *In a blender combine the flesh strawberries, light rum, fresh lime juice, simple syrup, and two handfuls of ice cubes. Blend until smooth.*

2. *Carefully pour the cocktail into chilled margarita glasses and garnish with a strawberry half.*

PREPARATION TIME:
10 minutes

GLASSWARE:
Margarita glass

CELEBRATION:
Anniversary

SERVES: 2

2 cups (340 g) fresh strawberries, hulled and sliced

4 ounces (120 ml) light rum

2 ounces (60 ml) fresh lime juice

1 ounce (30 ml) simple syrup (see recipe on page 40)

Ice cubes

GARNISH:
Strawberry half

GLITTERING COSMO

PREPARATION TIME:
5 minutes

GLASSWARE:
Pitcher and martini glass

CELEBRATION:
Night out

SERVES: 4

6 ounces (175 ml)
raspberry vodka

2 ounces (60 ml)
orange liqueur

2 ounces (60 ml)
fresh lemon juice

4 ounces (120 ml)
cranberry juice

2 to 3 pinches
of edible glitter

Ice cubes

GARNISH:
Lime wedge

THE GLITTERING COSMO is the ultimate cocktail for a fabulous girls' night out. This iconic pink drink, elevated with a touch of glitter, exudes glamour and fun, perfectly capturing the energy of the evening ahead.

Blending zesty cranberry, tangy lime, and smooth vodka, the Glittering Cosmo sets the stage for a night of dancing, laughter, and unforgettable memories. Whether sipped while getting glammed up or toasted on the dance floor, this cocktail adds a touch of sparkle to every moment.

1. *In a large pitcher, combine the raspberry vodka, orange liqueur, fresh lemon juice, cranberry juice, and 2 to 3 pinches of edible glitter.*

2. *Add enough ice cubes to fill the pitcher halfway and stir well to chill and mix the ingredients.*

3. *Pour the cocktail into chilled martini glasses.*

4. *Garnish each glass with a lime wedge.*

CINEMA SIPPER

ROLL OUT THE RED CARPET for the Cinema Sipper, a show-stopping pink foam cocktail that's the hero of the silver screen! With its irresistible taste and gorgeous looks, this drink is here to save any movie marathon with friends, turning a casual viewing into an unforgettable celebration.

Topped with a playful popcorn garnish on a cocktail stick, the Cinema Sipper blends indulgence with fun—offering the perfect mix of sip and snack. Whether you're watching a rom-com, an action-packed thriller, or a feel-good classic, this cocktail is sure to be the real blockbuster of the night.

1. *Combine the rum, pink grapefruit, grenadine syrup, simple syrup (see recipe on page 40), and egg white into a cocktail shaker along with a handful of ice cubes. Shake until cold and the egg white is frothy.*

2. *Strain the mixture into a chilled martini glass.*

3. *Carefully spear three pieces of popcorn with a cocktail stick and place across the rim of the martini glass.*

PREPARATION TIME:
10 minutes

GLASSWARE:
Coupe glass

CELEBRATION:
Movie night

SERVES: 1

1½ ounces (45 ml)
light rum

⅓ ounce (10 ml)
pink grapefruit juice

⅙ ounce (5 ml)
grenadine syrup

⅓ ounce (10 ml)
simple syrup
(see recipe on page 40)

⅓ ounce (10 ml) egg white

Ice cubes

GARNISH:
Popcorn on a cocktail stick

LOVE ON THE ROCKS

PREPARATION TIME:
5 minutes

GLASSWARE:
Rocks glass

CELEBRATION:
Breakups

SERVES: 1

2 ounces (60 ml)
bourbon or rye whiskey

1 ounce (30 ml)
fresh lemon juice

¾ ounce (20 ml)
simple syrup
(see recipe on page 40)

½ ounce (15 ml)
raspberry liqueur

A dash of bitters,
such as Angostura

Ice cubes

GARNISH:
Fresh raspberries and a
lemon twist

LOVE ON THE ROCKS IS THE PERFECT COCKTAIL to help start mending a broken heart. A blend of warming bourbon, bitters, and fruity raspberry liqueur, it's strong enough to match the intensity of heartbreak yet soothing and uplifting. Whether you're in the process of healing or simply need a moment to reflect, grab your favorite takeout, queue up some Taylor Swift, and sip on this comforting concoction. With every swig, remember, heartbreak may hurt now, but it won't last forever.

1. *Place the rocks glass in a freezer to chill while you prepare the drink.*

2. *Combine the bourbon (or rye), lemon juice, simple syrup (see recipe on page 40), raspberry liqueur, and bitters in a cocktail shaker along with a handful of ice cubes and shake vigorously until the mixture is cool.*

3. *Carefully strain the mixture into the chilled rocks glass filled with fresh ice.*

4. *Garnish the cocktail with a fresh raspberry and a lemon twist.*

HOME SWEET HOME

ONCE ALL THE HEAVY LIFTING IS DONE and the cardboard boxes are finally unpacked, it's time to celebrate your new chapter in style. Home Sweet Home is the perfect cocktail to mark the occasion, filling your space with warmth, joy, and a well-earned sense of accomplishment. With the comforting flavors of crisp apple cider, smooth rum, and a touch of cinnamon, this drink wraps you in the cozy essence of home.

As the aromatic scent of cinnamon drifts through your new space, it sets the stage for calm, contentment, and the excitement of new beginnings. Whether you're toasting with friends, family, or just enjoying a quiet moment to yourself, this inviting cocktail is a delicious way to celebrate your fresh start. Take a sip, kick back, and let the sweet taste of Home Sweet Home welcome you to the next chapter of your life!

1. *In a small saucepan, warm the apple cider over low heat. Add the cinnamon sticks and cloves, and let it simmer for a few minutes until fragrant. Remove from heat once it's hot but not boiling.*

2. *In a glass mug, combine the dark rum, lemon juice, and honey syrup (see recipe on page 41). Top up with the warmed apple cider and stir gently to combine.*

3. *Drop the cinnamon stick into the mug for added warmth and aroma and garnish with a lemon slice and star anise.*

PREPARATION TIME:
10 minutes

GLASSWARE:
Glass mugs

CELEBRATION:
Housewarming

SERVES: 1

4 ounces (120 ml) apple cider

1 cinnamon stick

1 clove

1 ounce (30 ml) dark rum

½ ounce (15 ml) fresh lemon juice

½ ounce (15 ml) honey syrup (see recipe on page 41)

GARNISH:
Lemon slice, cinnamon stick, and star anise

TEATIME TONIC

PREPARATION TIME:
5 minutes

GLASSWARE:
Teacup

CELEBRATION:
Afternoon tea

SERVES: 1

3 ounces (90 ml)
Earl Grey tea (cooled to
room temperature)

1½ ounces (45 ml)
botanical gin

½ ounce (15 ml)
simple syrup
(see recipe on page 40)

½ ounce (15 ml)
fresh lemon juice

Ice cubes

Crushed ice

GARNISH:
Lemon slices and
edible flower

THIS COCKTAIL IS THE PERFECT BLEND of whimsy and refreshment, ideal for toasting with friends during a delightful afternoon tea served alongside a generous portion or two of cake!

This delightful cocktail combines the timeless sophistication of Earl Grey tea with the smooth botanicals of gin and a refreshing splash of citrus burst from the fresh lemon. Served in a charming cup and saucer, this elegant drink elevates any gathering to a special occasion. So, raid your grandma's china cabinet, get creative, and amaze guests with this classy cocktail concoction.

1. *Brew a strong cup of Earl Grey tea, then allow it to cool to room temperature.*

2. *Combine the Earl Grey tea, gin, lemon juice, and simple syrup (see recipe on page 40) in a cocktail shaker along with a handful of ice cubes and shake vigorously until the mixture is cool.*

3. *Carefully strain the mixture into a decorative teacup of crushed ice.*

4. *Garnish with a lemon slice and an edible flower for a lovely, delicate touch.*

PROMOTION POTION

LIFE'S MILESTONES deserve a proper celebration, and promotions are no exception! Too often, we shy away from celebrating our hard-earned victories—but not this time. Raise a glass of the Promotion Potion as the signature cocktail to toast this well-deserved opportunity, a sparkling twist on the classic passion fruit martini, crafted for those moments when your dedication and grit pay off.

Raise your glass to the passion and determination that got you here. Let the vibrant burst of passion fruit mirror your ambition, while the fizz of sparkling wine adds the perfect touch of glamour to your success. As you level up in your career, skip the modesty and toast in style with the Promotion Potion—a cocktail that's as bold and brilliant as your achievements.

1. *Scoop the seeds from the passion fruits into the can of a cocktail shaker.*

2. *Next add the vodka, passion fruit liqueur, lime juice and passion fruit syrup (see recipe on page 43).*

3. *Combine with a handful of ice cubes and shake vigorously until the mixture is cool.*

4. *Strain the mixture into two chilled martini glasses.*

5. *Top each glass with a shot of prosecco and garnish with a half of passion fruit.*

PREPARATION TIME:
5 minutes

GLASSWARE:
Martini glass and a shot glass

CELEBRATION:
Promotion

SERVES: 2

2 ripe passion fruits

2 ounces (60 ml) vanilla vodka

1 ounce (30 ml) passion fruit liqueur

½ ounce (15 ml) fresh lime juice

½ ounce (15 ml) passion fruit syrup (see recipe on page 43)

Ice cubes

Prosecco (or sparkling wine)

GARNISH:
Halved passion fruit

Acknowledgments

THANK YOU to Georgie Glass for her photography, which has helped bring the recipes to life, and to Sarah Hancox for her cocktail styling, which has added the perfect finishing touch to each drink. Your work has been essential in bringing this book together.

About the Author

RHIANNON LEE is a cocktail enthusiast and author from Yorkshire, England, with a passion for crafting the perfect drink for every occasion. With a PhD in chemistry, Rhiannon combines her scientific knowledge with hands-on experience from working in bars to fund her studies, allowing her to explore the art of flavor and perfect taste combinations. She has previously published a series of themed cocktail books, showcasing her expertise in pairing the right cocktail with the right moment.

INDEX